ONE WOMAN,
THREE PRISONS

The Rise Within the Ranks
June 1966 -June 2000

JO ANN M. MERTENS

DEDICATION

This book is first dedicated to my son, Dr. C. J. Mertens; his wife, Rhonda; granddaughters Ashley and Shelby; and my new great granddaughter, Haylee. I must not forget my late mother, Mary E. Mertens. She helped shape my life; she also helped me raise my son and was with me through every crisis in my life. My family is my reason for living.

This book is also dedicated to the late William R. Turner, who helped me move through the ranks. Also included with him are all of my friends and corrections co-workers. My story could not have been possible had it not been for their loyalty and support.

The book is dedicated to all persons who have worked in a correctional setting, including those who laid down their lives for others in the field.

This book is also dedicated to all the offenders I worked with over the years. Their plight made me want to go to work every day.

I salute those persons above who gave meaning to the corrections profession and helped mold the person I am today.

Finally, I want to dedicate this to family, co-workers, supervisors, friends, and all those people who think they know me. I hope they see the low points and highlights of my life which makes me who I am.

ACKNOWLEDGEMENTS

My son, Dr. C. J. Mertens, and his family, because they are my life.

Delbert Boone, motivational speaker, President of NND, Inc. for allowing me to use his story and picture.

My friend, M. Ross of Jefferson City, Missouri, for allowing me to share part of her story.

Beverly (Turner) Gardner for giving me permission to use her dad's (The Boss) pictures and stories in the book.

Sherry Boylan, Chesbay 360, for her excellent photography of my plaques.

S. Bruno, substance abuse counselor and journalist, for her advice and guidance.

My friends, Sandy and Mary for doing my footwork in Missouri.

Mark Schrieber, Jefferson City, Missouri, for his expertise in the beginning of my project.

The Major, who was with me through almost everything in corrections.

My friend, Linda, (now deceased) who befriended me at CMCC.

My friend, Marion, who always gave me a "prison tour."

CHAPTERS

PRE-CORRECTIONS

Early Years to 1966

I cannot tell the story of my life working in the Missouri prison system without giving some background on myself. I grew up in a small river town in mid-Missouri. My father's family was all German, and my mother's side of the family was a mix of Scotch and Irish. I went to a small parochial school with only two classrooms. After graduation from eighth grade, I went on to the small public high school of a little over a hundred students. I took the usual courses.

When I was five years old, my father was killed in a dump truck accident. If he had lived, my story might have been different. I knew he loved me because he was responsible for completing my entire baby book. I remember my father reading comic books to me every night. I learned to read early because of the comic books. By today's standards, I lived in a dysfunctional family, but I didn't know that. After my father died, Mom and I lived in the large old house of my German ancestors. It was stately and beautiful, the oldest house in town. It was paid for, so there were no house payments. My mom received a small stipend for me from my father's employer. At that time, apparently, there was no Social Security.

Grandma and my unmarried aunt lived there also. My mom and grandmother did not get along well, but Mom had no choice.

She was thirty-four years old when I was born. Women had little choice of employment. She was a factory worker all of her life, an excellent, hardworking employee who took no sick time. It was from my mother I learned my work ethic. That work ethic, I believe, was also passed on to my son and his children. She was the stability in my life. My grandmother died when I was ten years old, so I had to fend for myself during the summer while Mom was working. My aunt did nothing to help me. I do believe Mom and I grew stronger because of the life we lived. Mom and I fought the world together and no woman was ever stronger than my thin little mama.

After Grandma died, no one was worried about who owned the house. It actually belonged to me and my aunt. Mom put plumbing in the house. She got me my first bicycle. I was obese during my childhood. Genes may have played a part but I feel being alone so much made me eat more. The German tradition was also to clean your greasy plate at each meal.

In high school I had few dreams of the future, but I was always drawn to the downtrodden. When I was in grade school, I was walking down the street when a very old black man, highly respected in our small community, was coming toward me. He moved off the sidewalk for me—a child. I was very uncomfortable with this. I ran home to ask my mother about it and she had no answer for me.

I was fortunate enough to be presented with a small scholarship to a college near Kansas City, Missouri. I thought about accepting it, but I had friends who had already moved to St. Louis to work as clerical staff. I wanted my independence. I made the decision to move to the big city and forgo college for immediate money. I moved in with my friends. The city was fascinating but scary—the crime rate was high. One of my friends was almost pulled into a car as we were walking. I immediately got a job with a bank. It was a boring job. I was the youngest in my section and the other women babied me.

I wanted a car most of all. A car in my driveway has been a very important issue for me. My mother had sold my dad's car after he died, and we always had to depend on others for transportation. When I had $250 saved, I bought a 1952 Chevy for exactly that. I didn't even have my license yet, so my cousin drove us back and forth to St. Louis. I later got my license and never looked back.

A few months later, I was offered a clerical job at St. Louis City Welfare (now the Department of Social Services). I jumped at the chance because of the better pay and benefits. Everyone wanted a state job. This was the first time I had worked with more blacks than whites. It was very different for me, but I soon learned the culture. I was excited also because if I worked there long enough I could become a caseworker without a degree. I would then be working in the slums of the city of St. Louis, and it was fascinating to me. As I took the bus downtown, I passed through the poorest sections of the city. I began to realize what poverty was all about.

When I was working at St. Louis City Welfare--now Social Services, I met the mother of the famous R&B singer Solomon Burke (now deceased). I enjoyed the new experiences of city life for the first time.

I finally felt free of the rural area I grew up in. After a year, though, several of my girlfriends moved back to mid-Missouri. We had been living in a place where we were afraid to come in and out of the apartment, which was on West Pine Street near Kings Highway. Coming back after a weekend away, we would wait for a long time before we had courage to run into the house; driving through the city, we had problems with young guys trying to get in our car. A woman had been raped in the house next door.

I finally gave in. I transferred to the state welfare building in Jefferson City. I did miss the city life. Work was very dull in the state office building. While working in my boring clerical job, I became a single mother. My own mother moved from her home in Chamois, Missouri, to help me with my son. At age fifty-six, she was hired in what was called a political clerical position, a job my cousin helped her to get. She had only been a factory worker but she thrived in this position and worked there ten years. I knew from my early twenties that I couldn't work as clerical staff and support my son, but I now had no money to go to college.

Jefferson City had seven prisons in the area and the Department of Corrections was one of the largest employers in the city. I passed the famous Missouri State Penitentiary (MSP) every day on my way to work. I would look at those guard towers and the large rock wall and wonder what was really behind the wall. It was fascinating. I wondered what it would be like to work there.

MSP Gas Chamber

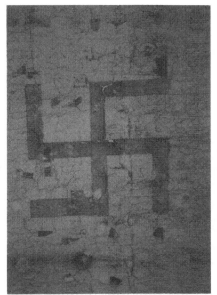

Swastika on Cell Wall, MSP　　　　Housing Unit, MSP

Wall and Guard Tower, MSP

MISSOURI STATE PENITENTIARY

1966–1974

After several years of working for the Department of Welfare, I received an interview for an upgraded clerical position at MSP. The promotion would be more money for my son and me. I went to the interview with butterflies in my stomach. I even asked the interviewer if it was all right that I was a single mother. I was not sure they would want me to be around male inmates. What a crazy, shameful feeling I had about myself. The interviewer looked at me with surprise; I don't think he even realized what I was asking. I got the job.

I started working at MSP in the mid-sixties, in the mail room of the penitentiary. The mail room was "inside" and separate from the administrative offices. It was something new to hire a woman for this position, because at that time, no woman went down inside the institution. The male staff of the mail room had to bring my work to me. There were constant remarks by the male staff that I was being coddled.

My desk was outside the warden's office. Working outside the warden's office was interesting to me. I saw all the big shots of corrections and the state go in and out. I observed the first wedding ever held in the prison. I had watched the romance through the letters we had to read—the couple was Ben and his sweet Jeanie. The ceremony was performed in the warden's office with his secretary as a witness. I watched the blood tests being performed. He wore his prison clothing and Jeanie had a nice dress. The prison provided fresh flowers but no guests were permitted. The prison chaplain performed the ceremony. After I left MSP, I am not sure what happened to the couple.

MSP was built in the 1800s so everything in it was old, but it had the highest level of security in the state of Missouri. The inmates who worked in the administration building were trustees who had long sentences but had earned trust of the administration. Most of them were in for murder. I had to ride up in the old elevator with a trustee. One day, he came in with fresh flowers for the warden's office. He first offered the flowers to me. I knew I must not react the wrong way or my career would be gone. I graciously thanked him but said no. This inmate called me "Miss Jo Ann." No first names were ever used for women unless the title "Miss" was added. The inmate would go immediately to administrative segregation (total lockdown). If I was to survive both staff and inmates, I had to learn the lessons early.

Even some of the other female employees seemed to resent me. I don't know why. One walked through my office with the roster of inmates and said, "There's an inmate here named Mertens. Is that your husband?" I checked the rosters—there had never been an inmate with that name. I knew I had to have my back because no one else would.

We had to read every letter coming in and going out of the prison and check them all for contraband. One letter sent out by an inmate had his pulled teeth in it. Women sent in letters with perfume, powder, and pubic hairs. The work was a bit gross.

I remember two specific incidents. I had been reading the letters of a young man who had lost his girlfriend, and it was obvious he was very despondent. I informed my boss about this, but nothing was done. This man was a trustee, and he had a job outside the walls. He escaped and was not found for several years. A woman must use her God-given ability. She must trust her gut. It has never failed me. I also read disturbing letters from a young man to his family. He kept saying he was being raped by the other inmates, and he asked his family to help him. Being a country girl, I asked how that could happen. The male staff really got a laugh out of my ignorance. Another lesson learned.

In the mail room, there was an inmate named Van who was our runner (he cleaned and did any work we asked him to do). I liked him. He was so excited because he was to be getting out soon. When he was released we were all happy for him. Months later, I was reading a newspaper called the *St. Louis Whirl*. The *Whirl* reports all the crime in the ghettos of St. Louis—it has been in existence for years, and it is something else. Many inmates subscribed to it. I always read it. I opened it one day and saw Van's picture covering the whole front of the paper; he had been shot to death that week. Some things you never get used to.

I was learning quickly how to survive in an environment of males only. One day, an old sergeant came to the mail room. He asked me to weigh a package, so we went into the back room where the scales were located. As I was bending over, he popped my bra strap. I whirled around and told him never to do that again. He seemed very surprised but backed off. Because he outranked me, I could have lost my job, but I didn't care. He never bothered me again.

After some months, the mail room was moved to the third floor of the administration building, so they could hire more women. The move was good for me because the men did not resent me as much. They did not have to bring my work to me. Another plus of being moved to the third floor was that I didn't have to put up with the department director close behind my desk breathing down my neck. I had to be tolerant of the big boss and still hold my ground. I knew I could move up in the corrections field because it was the *right time* for women in corrections. I also knew there were few ways to do it: stand up to the men and gain their respect or go another route. One was "sleeping with the enemy". I chose to become very assertive, and it worked. I gradually gained the respect of the male staff and the inmates.

Two years after I started working at MSP, the warden approached me about working in the visiting room—definitely a promotion for me. My new title was corrections matron (ugh) because female staff were not yet corrections officers. There was only one corrections matron at MSP. All the others worked at the female institution in Tipton, Missouri. I had to take a written merit test, which was given for all positions under the state merit system. The test consisted of questions about cooking, sewing, and dealing with female inmates. I was afraid I had flunked it because those areas were not my forte. I passed and was promoted to corrections matron. The substantial pay increase certainly helped with raising my son. I worked every other weekend and had every Monday off with a three-day weekend every other week. This did not add up to forty hours every week, but I didn't worry about it, although I did regret that my mother had to babysit my son so often on weekends. He was happy, though. She let him tear up her apartment and play scientist.

As a part-time corrections matron, I sometimes worked in the classification office. In that section there was a huge vault, which contained cabinets with the inmate files. I tried not to stay long in this area because I found it bothersome and creepy. Along all sides of the vault were pictures of inmates who had been put to death at MSP. I would look at their faces and wonder what they had been like. More than half were black. There was one woman's picture there. Her name was Bonny Heady. She and Austin Hall were involved in the Greenlease kidnapping/murder in Kansas City, Missouri in 1953.

Picture of Inmates Put to Death in Gas Chamber

The visiting room was very dark and dank. It was rectangular. A heavy screen separated the family from the inmates and there were stools on both sides. I watched the visitors. An officer was on the other side of the screen to monitor the inmates from administrative segregation. There was an outside room where minimum-security inmates could visit their families. I was responsible for both areas. I loved working on weekends, because other than the front gate officer, I was alone to make my own decisions. The upper-level administrative staff rarely came in on weekends. I once had to testify in a trial of an inmate because he passed contraband (illegal items) in the visiting room. I was very nervous when I knew I had to testify. Before the trial, the warden said, "Make us proud, Jo Ann." I answered I would tell the truth. We won the case.

The woman I relieved in the visiting room had been there a long time. She was much older than I was and thought I was too young to work in the position. Each time I saw her she would tell me they (the inmates) really put one over on me because she found holes in the screen. I began to pay much more attention to the screen. I made sure it was perfect before I left the room. The last time she told me there was a hole, I said, "If there's a hole, you put it there." No more problems.

The visiting room was interesting. I met serial killers and their families. I met a police officer and his wife who visited their son, who was in for murder. The parents were great people. I remember one inmate who was known for eating light bulbs. He always lay on the floor in the visiting room. His family could not make him get up. The minimum security visiting room was for inmates who lived outside the walls with more privileges. They could visit without the screen. You had to be very vigilant with the minimum security inmates. They did many things they should not do, and could not have done, in the screened visiting room. Their actions were very hard to catch. Many visitors were nice, but some had attitudes. I tried to deal with everyone fairly.

One day I found the male officer sleeping in the visiting room on the inmate side. I tried and tried to wake him up from the other side of the screen. I gave up, but the lieutenant on duty found him. I received the worst verbal warning of my career for not notifying the lieutenant of the situation.

One of the highlights of my career took place in the visiting room. When I was not working in the visiting room, I floated to any place I was needed. I learned to work many jobs, and this was to my advantage. One of them was the switchboard. When I was working there, I read in the St. Louis paper the wife of one of the inmates I knew well was wanted for bank robbery. A few weeks later, she came into the visiting room as if nothing had happened. I called the deputy warden, who in turn called the state patrol. She was indeed wanted for bank robbery. The patrol came (male, of course) and arrested her. I had to do a strip and cavity search on her in an office. There were no rules about cavity searches and no gloves. That soon changed. As I was searching her, I ran my fingers through her hair and her wig came off. At the top of her head, was a small bit of hair and through the hair was a knife. She gave it up peacefully but my heart was racing. For that incident, I received my first commendation.

Be mindful there was no formal training at that time; it was on-the-job training. By the time I could go to a training program, I went to the advanced level, because I refused to go through basic training after eleven years on the job. I tied for the top score. All of my training in the field is listed at the end of the book.

I had to pat-search the women who came in, and I also checked their purses. Male visitors emptied their pockets. I was so excited when I found a small container with light brown powder in it—I was sure I had found some type of dope. I asked the front door officer about it. He laughed and said that was snuff. Another lesson learned.

At this point, I would like to speak about my opinion of drugs in prisons and in general. Drug addiction accounts for many people being sent to prison, but it is not the root cause of their problems in life. Most people who are on drugs are taking them to hide their pain. I firmly believe that the use of drugs is directly connected to something that happened during a person's formative years. It could be bad parenting, peer influence, heredity, or specific painful incidents.

Some people are actually genetically predisposed to addiction. Although some experts say drug use or sales are not violent crimes—and I guess you could say that is true—when people are under the influence of any drug or mood-altering substance, they may commit violent crimes. We wonder if locking them up helps. Sometimes it does; sometimes nothing helps. I have known several inmates who died, either directly or indirectly, because of drug use. The crucial words—jails, institutions, or death—hold true. And remember what drug use does to the addict's family and children.

Mental health self-medicating is also a factor. I see this more with today's youth. There are constantly new terms; for example, a new one to me is impulse control disorder. I feel some of the problems are created by improper or no discipline at home and an "it's all about me" attitude the young people have today. When talking with inmates about drugs, I always encouraged them to feel their pain and cope with it. Later in the book, you will read about a young inmate who did just that and was set free.

Prisons are a breeding ground for illegal substances. Hooch, or home brew, was constantly found. This could be made easily with almost any fermented food. The smell was one you did not forget. Near our prison farms in the early years, marijuana and locoweed grew freely, and the inmates knew how to find both. Drugs had strange ways of getting into a prison. Unfortunately, staff were sometimes conned into bringing it in. Girlfriends and wives brought drugs in to the inmates. These women were very clever in hiding the drugs in their mouths, on their children, or in their body parts. There were special cells for an inmate to wait in until he had passed the heroin or cocaine balloon he had swallowed. As an officer at MSP, I had to go to RCC (then still a satellite) to search children and a baby. There were no female officers at RCC until 1974. A family was believed to be bringing in drugs. The search of the children was very hard for me but I tried to be as professional as possible. I found no drugs.

Drugs could be thrown over a fence or outside a fence. Cocaine was sent sometimes under a stamp on a letter. Deals were set up from outside the prison and sometimes inside the prison. If there was a way to bring drugs in, the inmates would figure it out. The staff learned many of the tricks but still missed some. In drug deals, one inmate would "jigger" (be the lookout) for another.

Prison language was fascinating. When your release date was near you were "short" and you had a number of days and a "wake up or a get up". Drugs had many names. Here's a partial list of some of my favorite, creative jargon used by inmates. An "OG" was an older inmate—an old gangsta— who knew the ropes. They were usually respected. "Square people" were staff. The "streets" usually meant outside the prison. If you had a court charge you "caught a case." If you "copped a plea" you admitted to a lesser crime. This phrase could also be used for violations heard within the institution. "Fresh meat" referred to a new first offender arriving at the prison. The one I thought was funny was "kicking the bo-bo," which is simply meaningless talk. We all used the word "kite" which was an illegal note being passed or even a letter to the staff. "Snow man" was a drug dealer. Getting a "ticket" meant receiving a conduct violation. All inmates had nicknames, and they were very creative in naming the staff. One officer and his son worked together. Their names were "Boots" and "Shoes." I never knew what my nickname was, but I know I had one. There were many other slang words, and they varied from region to region. I enjoyed figuring out why the slang word was used. A prison is a society like no other, with a language all its own, just as many young people have today.

This story still haunts me today. I was working the visiting room on a weekend with only the front gate officer there with me. A very old black man came in with a bag carrying his toothbrush and a few other personal items. He had been released not long before after serving many years on a life sentence. His family and friends were all gone. Prison life was all he knew. After many years in prison or coming back numerous times makes a person "institutionalized." This means prison life is all you know and it is home. This old man begged both of us to let him come back in. I had to tell him we could not accept him at MSP if he had not committed another crime. The old man walked out with his head hanging down. Both of us felt very bad for this senior. We wondered if the prison system was working. Still, I had to do what I had to do. I will never forget this incident. I wondered what happened to this senior on the streets. Now we have developed geriatric wards in many of our maximum security prisons. How many years does it take to pay for a crime? I will never know. I do know the job for us in criminal justice is first to protect the public. It is the most important goal.

One incident of terrible degradation was told to me by a man I worked with. I never doubted his story. It took place at MSP before I left in 1974. One evening a group of inmates were causing problems in a housing unit. A high-ranking official at that time ordered all of the troublemakers to administrative segregation (total lockup). As the armed officers watched, the inmates had to strip naked and crawl on hands and knees, nose to butt, to the administrative segregation unit. This official showed no mercy to the majority of the inmates. The person who told this story was a part of the armed cadre. He did not approve of these actions, but to hold a job, you had to disregard your beliefs and do what you were told. The courts and inmate lawsuits now play a part in what happens in prisons.

One particular captain on duty was very annoying. He would come in the visiting room and knead my arm or neck. I had to get up and walk to avoid him. Please remember that laws against sexual harassment didn't exist at this time. I could be rich today if the laws had been there and enforceable. My solution was to have the front gate officer notify me when the captain was on his way. I remained standing. I was taller than he was. The problem was solved.

My family was no stranger to corrections. Before my time, my uncle was working in a tower when James Earl Ray escaped. He failed to shoot quickly enough. Ray escaped and you know the rest. My uncle was suspended but did not lose his job. Another uncle quit after the bloody, fiery riot in 1954. I also had one cousin who put in many years.

Once, shortly after I started, my uncle was visiting my family when I received a phone call from one of the good-looking, married captains. He welcomed me to MSP. I told my uncle how nice the captain was. My uncle told me never to talk to this captain again—that he was a ladies' man and no good. I later found this to be true. I advised many women on how to handle him. He was later sued several times for sexual harassment. He and I got along well, because I put him in his place in the beginning. He came to me to talk about his conquests. If my uncle had not warned me, I may have fallen victim to his charms. There was a very small group of men who preyed on any new, unsuspecting female employee who was vulnerable. He was the worst of the lot.

There were several interesting differences between men and women in corrections in the seventies. About a year after I started as a matron, the corrections officers were given a large raise. When I did not get the raise, I went to my boss and was told *only the men* got it. Oh, if I had only known. A few years (1973) later, we two corrections matrons were actually made corrections officers, equal to the male officers. Another woman tried to claim she was the first female officer in corrections but was made an officer later than I was. She was a friend of the warden and hidden somewhere by management at that time. This can be verified in a corrections book called *Somewhere in Time*. My name is in the book and my picture is also in Jefferson City Correctional Center on a wall honoring past employees.

A different sort of harassment took place when I worked the switch board part-time. On my break, I would go to the break room to visit with other workers. In 1973, a very progressive, well-known man from New York came to work as division director. I had read about him. On one of my breaks, I remarked that I felt a black man would be put in a high-ranking position by this new director, although I had no inside information. The very next day, I was removed from my part-time job at the switchboard with no explanation. When I tried to find one, no one would answer.

I finally went to the division director (before the new director was appointed) prepared with information. He denied I was removed for mentioning a black being promoted. I told him I would be put back on the switchboard or I would go to the media to tell some of the things I knew (many are not mentioned in this book). He said, "Now, we are both from Osage County." I said, "I'm now a resident of Cole County." The next day the warden came to me and said I was back on the switchboard. He suggested that we should forgive and forget. I answered, "I'll forgive, but I'll never forget." Somehow my assertiveness did gain respect for me, but it's a shame I had to use threats to be treated fairly at that time.

Another incident was with the parking of cars. Each morning many of us double-parked to wait for a spot until the midnight shift staff got off duty. One morning I was waiting for a parking spot. A police officer made me move. I later called the police station. I found the deputy warden had reported only me. I always checked a situation out, because I knew there was an explanation.

This was the same person who later became warden. He was hated by some and loved by others. It's very hard to describe this deputy made warden. He walked to the beat of his own drummer. He had no thoughts about rehabilitation. He just wanted MSP to run without bad press and he wanted to satisfy his own ego. He had his favorite inmates. One was the officers' barber. One day while I was working the visiting room, the inmate barber came up to me. He said he was getting out soon, and he needed someone to show him the town. I felt trapped, because I knew I could not report him or I would have problems with the deputy warden. I thought for a moment and then said, "If you mean me, and you show up at my door, I will call the police." No more problems.

It is ironic to me that after I moved to Virginia, I met Delbert Boone, a motivational speaker who now counsels inmates and other people. He is very good at what he does. He tells it as the addicts need to hear it. He had done time (was an inmate) at MSP at the same time I was working there for that same warden. He, as an inmate, and I, as an officer, had many of the same feelings about this high-ranking official. We enjoyed our talk very much. He is certainly a success story.

Delbert Boone and Author

Don't believe everything was bad at MSP. I met and became friends with some wonderful people. I learned to respect many of the inmates on their terms, not on what they did. The worst thing to do was read a file, because many were unbelievable and violent, and I didn't want it to taint my treatment of the inmates. "Fair, firm, and consistent" was a rule I learned to live by. I also learned to walk by the inmates, look them straight in the eye, and speak to them. This prevented many of the catcalls and obscene language. It didn't work with all of them, but it did with many.

On the other hand, I probably did not realize how dangerous living or working there was. Many inmates I knew were killed while serving their sentences. A lieutenant and a sergeant were stabbed to death while working their shifts. I'd worked with both of them. They were very good officers and did not deserve to die. These things made staff hardened. Everyone thinks of the military or the police as being killed in the line of duty, but at the Missouri State Capitol building in Jefferson City, overlooking the river, is a memorial to law enforcement, including corrections staff, who were killed in the line of duty. I knew several of the people whose names are listed there.

One person who was partially responsible for my rise in corrections was called Bill by many of his corrections friends. In the music world, he was known as "Billy Bob." Inmates called him "the Major". I met him when I worked the visiting room at MSP. I would call him at the control center to have the inmates brought to the visiting room. He was a lieutenant (at that time) who was well respected by all staff and was a very nice person who knew how to run his station—the control center. The control center is the hub of any institution.

Bill Turner

When I started in corrections, Missouri State Penitentiary was the main institution and the others were only satellites, all under the control of the warden. When the new director came, he promoted this lieutenant to be an administrative assistant to the warden. The new director also began breaking barriers for blacks in the Department of Corrections (DOC). (My gut was right)

Bill had to share an office with his secretary. I saw this woman move her desk so it would not face this black man. When he came in, he turned the office upside down, and she did face him. He was determined, as I was, to make gender and race situations equal for all.

In February 1974, Bill was promoted to major. The new director had decided to make each institution a separate entity, no longer under the warden. The director chose the new major to head an institution which would be called Renz Correctional Center (RCC). It was formerly Renz Farm, named after Paul V. Renz who had owned the property before selling it to the state. This was literally a farm with a dormitory-type building on the property, housing minimum-security male inmates.

The major picked a team of experienced employees to accompany him to start this new institution. I was one of the team members and in many ways, saw this to be a great opportunity for promotion. I also wanted to move away from the politics of MSP, so I accepted the offer. Before I left MSP, the major found a replacement for me. I trained the first black female officer in a male institution. There were some conflicting stories saying she was the first female officer at MSP, but I have in my position the proof she was not. She worked there successfully for many years and was respected by all.

I had worked at MSP for eight years by that time, as both a mail room clerk and a corrections officer. I had broken two barriers for women at one of the toughest prisons west of the Mississippi. I did reminisce a bit. I thought of the prison band named the Versatiles. They were hand-picked to go into the community to entertain. I love hearing that music. I met Willie Nelson personally when he played for the inmates at MSP.

This was not the place to work for everyone. One man worked for one day and resigned because of the constant clanging of the gates. The smells of food, cleaning materials, and even unwashed bodies; and the sounds of those gates are hard to forget. The motivational speaker, Delbert Boone, and I talked about the specific traits of a prison. He and I agreed on all of these traits which only people who have been associated with institutions could share. I remember going for a ride on the warden's golf cart for an up-close-and-personal tour. I went into the gas chamber several times but never witnessed an execution. I was told it was memorable but the memories were not good. Bill Turner relayed these feelings to me and others—he had witnessed several executions. He said you would never forget the experience.

The hospital of the prison was a very depressing place to go. I only went there when necessary. One day a young man drank Magic Shave. At the time, there was no antidote. Places all over the nation were called to try to find an antidote to save him. He died. I'm sure there were inmates with AIDS there but it had not yet been diagnosed. In my later AIDS training, I remarked this would be something big—I had no idea how big. Once I was walking down the hospital corridor when an arm suddenly reached out to me. I was afraid but found the person was a mentally challenged inmate who had made the hospital his home.

I recall being introduced to Sonny Liston, the famous boxer, who had been an inmate there. He came back to talk to the population. He was huge; his hand looked like a ham. My hand was lost in his. It was nice to meet famous people without all of the hoopla surrounding them.

When I worked in the visiting room, I received meals made by the inmates in L-Hall. It was a minimum-security dormitory right outside the prison walls. These meals were delicious. I enjoyed the fresh blackberry cobbler. Down inside at the big mess hall was a different story. You never knew what you were eating, and I seldom ate there. Women had to be escorted by a male staff member to eat there. One young woman was grabbed by an inmate with mental health problems. He was soon overpowered, but that incident reinforced the rule of escorts. Today women walk everywhere and work every post.

Bill spearheaded the desegregation of the housing units in the 1970s, because it was realistic to have a black ranking officer lead this powerful move. The emergency squad went in, but there was no trouble at all. The inmates adjusted better than expected. Of course, individuals had problems with their roomies. All of the rest of us watched from afar. We were stressed because of what might happen to our colleagues. It was a time of great anticipation.

All of these memories came rushing back to me as I prepared to leave MSP after eight years. I was now in my early thirties. I had learned much about living that many people will never know. The experiences were incredible. Still, I loved the work and the adrenaline rush it gave me to just come in every morning. I knew very early I had found my life's work and challenges. I was never afraid of the inmates but was always cautious.

When I started at DOC, a college degree was not necessary. Sometime during my stay at MSP, the federal government initiated LEEP grants, which entitled corrections staff to work on a degree. Tuition and books were paid for. I jumped at the chance. I went to school two nights per week, taking all my criminal justice courses first. I went to college at Lincoln University (historically black college) which had a past of its own. I received a commendation from the criminal justice advisor for excellence in all my classes. I loved going to school again after ten years, but working all day, going to school at night, and caring for my son became too stressful. When I made the decision to transfer to RCC, I dropped out of college. This may have been a big mistake in my life; however, my son was nine years old. He and my mother needed me at home. I feel I made the right decision. Sometimes you have to make sacrifices for the greater good of the family.

RENZ CORRECTIONAL CENTER

1974–1982

In April 1974, our team moved to RCC. There were already custody and other staff there; however, we were the ones who would build an entirely new institution. When I came there, I was shocked. It was still definitely a man's world. I found out later there were three psychologists and a clerical person (she is still a friend of mine) pushed into a small office in the basement. We were packed like sardines. One of the psychologists is now the department director. I worked on the first floor from the control center with my boss, the business manager and his secretary, the lieutenant in charge of custody, and a few inmates. There was one bathroom with no lock. When I used it, a male officer would have to stand outside the door. I finally insisted a lock be installed. The control center inmate was a handful. He resented me because I reorganized all of his work. He developed a bad attitude, and he finally had to be removed.

In October 1974, I was promoted to Corrections Officer II (Sergeant). I was the first female to hold this position in a male institution. This was another barrier broken, but it was not without backlash. I heard many rumors—theories about why I got the position. Many thought as a woman, I could not do the job. Several of the long-term male corrections officers thought it should be theirs. I can't argue with their feelings, but I did compete fairly through the merit system.

Early on we had little equipment. One night there was an escape. I was positioned alone under the Missouri River Bridge with no weapon and a radio that did not work well. I had not yet learned the codes for the radio. I sat there all night waiting for the male inmate to pop up. I was finally relieved of my post early in the morning. Several years later, an escapee was caught in that same spot. What would I have done if he had come into my sight? I will never know.

Two disgusting things come to mind when I think about what some inmates will actually do. There was an inmate at RCC who worked in food service. He had some reason for wanting to spoil the food for everyone. He put his naked behind on a big steam kettle with a plan to defecate in the steam kettle. The joke was on him because he ended up in medical services with a badly burned behind before he could get the job done.

A gross thing happened to me personally at RCC when we had only female inmates. (This came later in the story.) I came in early one morning to work and was caught by the night captain. No female officers had yet come on day-shift duty. He asked me if I would strip-search a female inmate who had to go on a trip outside the institution fence. I told him it had been a long time. After his pleading, I gave in. I took the female inmate in a very small bathroom and asked her to "strip." One of the routine things we did was ask them to bend over and spread their cheeks. As she did that (imagine a very small room) she broke wind directly in my face. I was so furious I did not know what to do. I jumped back quickly. She apologized. She said she never intended to do that. How could I write a conduct violation when she claimed an accident? I knew better but let it go. I told the captain never to ask me to do that again in my position. I guess I took my frustrations out on him, but we did laugh. There was no point in staying upset. I am sure her friends got a laugh out of it, too. That's one of the less serious games inmates play. Staff expects the games.

When I first came to RCC, it was decided I needed a uniform like the male officers. I was allowed to design my own using the same material and color (green) as the male officers. I designed a light green shirt, a dark green vest, and dark green pants. I thought it was a great design because it was becoming to any woman in uniform. That didn't last long. When more women were hired, they had to wear the same uniforms as the men, which were very ill fitting as you might imagine, with gaping waists and baggy pants. Later, Corrections Industries (who made the uniforms) began to tailor some uniforms for women. I hope today they fit much better; I'm sure they do.

Early in RCC's inception as a separate institution, another female officer was hired. She was the wife of a captain at another institution. She was a perfect fit. She was strong, as I was, and it helped me to have a female colleague. The male inmates had become used to me by that time, so we had very few problems.

There was a male inmate who was big and strong, a weight lifter, and a good inmate. He respected the administration. I will call him Porky. Porky was an alcoholic and a robber, but he had a kind heart. He had been in and out of the prison system several times and was well known. I respected this man. He was known as OG (Old Gangsta), and he carried that title well. He made sure the young inmates were respectful to all of the staff—at least to our faces.

Another inmate ran the canteen (a store for inmates). He also helped us in the control center (the main hub of the institution). We all knew he ran the canteen his own way. He found ways to make some profits for himself, but he made the institution money so it was overlooked.

I had begun to read inmates' files, because of my position. When I read the file of the canteen inmate, I found he was on the end of a long sentence for killing two older women and raping them after they were dead. He would bring the staff popcorn at the control center. After reading the file, it took a while for me to put it all in perspective and go on as usual. I ate the popcorn like everyone else. He was released and never heard of again. The inmate named Porky was also released, but he will reappear in this book.

In a small institution, the staff and the inmates are very interactive. Unlike at MSP, I learned the names of almost all of them. At RCC, I learned about other cultures. I remember the Boss consoling a young girl in the visiting room. She was afraid of her parent being in prison. The Boss explained to her that the prison was like a town; he was the mayor, the officers were the city council, and the inmates were the residents of the town. This made the girl much more accepting.

At this small institution I began learning about gangs and radical religious groups. MSP and the larger institutions had more formal gangs from St. Louis and Kansas City, such as the Crips and the Bloods. I learned very quickly about the white supremacy groups such as the Aryan Brotherhood and the Sword, Arm, and Covenant of the Lord. Most were under the guise of religion. The Nation of Islam was peaceful and cooperative. It was accepted as a religion in the prison system. I learned much about the Koran from our control center clerk. It has similarities to the Bible. The Moorish Science Temple of America, on the other hand, was a very radical group, and the Department of Corrections (DOC) refused to give it religious status.

I met the very notorious leader of this group at RCC. I could see the hate for me in his eyes. He was from St. Louis and was known for major drug trafficking and murders. This man was one I was very cautious about. A St. Louis paper ran an article online saying the trial of this gangster was the longest criminal trial in St. Louis history, taking more than seven months. Six people were found guilty and were given very long sentences. This group of people was a front for a heroin-trafficking operation and claimed to control nearly half of the local cocaine trade. The leader was linked to a dozen drug-related murders. The drug ring allegedly began in 1978 and disbanded in 1992. This leader commanded his followers while he was in and out of prison.

Setting up a new institution took quite a bit of work. We had to set up a classification office with caseworkers, plus a business office, a chapel, holding cells, and many other programs. We had to revamp the maintenance department and food service. Our Boss was very progressive. We started to rely heavily on volunteers to help because of the lack of staff. A Christian group called "Prison Fellowship" (Chuck Colson started the group and had played a major role in the Watergate scandal) became a very strong force at RCC and other prisons. A canning building was turned into a beautiful gym. The upper area was classrooms and offices. A new era had begun for RCC.

We needed to have someone who was responsible for monitoring inmate release dates and checking validity of court papers. This person would also calculate "good time" that was given for extra work, including giving blood donations and flood time, which was the amount of days an inmate worked extra during a flood. The "good time" was taken off of the inmate's sentence. It was very popular. A record officer level one position became available. I applied for it and was promoted. It was sad to move out of custody. If I had continued in custody, I would have been required to work the midnight and evening shift, which would've taken precious time away from my son and me. I still remained an upper-level staff member at RCC. This was another barrier I broke, because I was the first female record officer in a male institution.

RCC was across the Missouri River from Jefferson City. It was situated in the "river bottom," which meant it was subject to flooding. Before I came to the institution, the inmates had had to be moved out several times. We were on flood alert more times than I could count. We had to monitor the river stages and be prepared to move inmates with little notice. We actually moved out several times, and finally in 1993, we had the five-hundred-year flood, which destroyed RCC. The great flood will be referred to later. Before that time, staff and inmates worked side by side to keep it together and clean it up. Most inmates assigned to RCC liked it there. They were willing to keep it going. My boss was determined to keep RCC in operation no matter what.

Things went fairly smoothly for over a year. We had the usual institutional problems—inmates driving the tractors sometimes took a trip to a liquor store nearby and got drunk. Marijuana and locoweed grew in the fields. We had to constantly monitor this situation. It was easy to drop drugs off in the fields or along the side of the road. RCC only had a barbed wire fence around it. I saw many inmates high on locoweed. They became very out of control.

We had a few fights but we were able to transfer those inmates back to the main penitentiary (MSP) or another institution. Working in corrections was good. During this period, the major was promoted to superintendent (they are now all called wardens or deputy wardens). No one at that time could be a warden other than the warden at MSP. Our little four-hundred-bed institution was now truly a separate institution from MSP.

In 1975, all hell broke loose. The superintendent of the female institution in Tipton, Missouri was stabbed by a female inmate and was nearly killed. Unrest spread across that institution. It housed women with all levels of security but was built as a minimum security institution. Early one morning our boss (now fondly called "the Boss") called the staff together. He had received a call from the central office stating that we would be receiving thirty-six female inmates before the end of the day. How would we accomplish this? We did. We had become a very close-knit team who could do anything we needed to do.

First, with the help of other institutions, a dormitory of male inmates was shipped to other places. I cannot begin to tell you what we had to do and the details we had to work out. It was total chaos. We prepared the housing unit as best we could. There were only two female staff (me, for one) who had worked custody. Policy and procedure had to be quickly written. We had no supplies for women. I certainly did not know what to expect. I had heard rumors that female inmates were very difficult to work with. The term "co-corrections" was a new name for RCC and the Department of Corrections. The mixing of male and female offenders had never been tried in Missouri before. Oh, what a night.

Late that evening the bus arrived. I had already told my family I was not sure when I would be home. As these thirty-six females came off the bus, my heart was in my throat. I had worked with male inmates, but I had only heard tales about the females. Now they were here. I had never seen such a group of big, ugly, scary women in my life. They were not happy with the move. Cursing came out of almost every mouth. We knew we were getting the worst, but I'd never thought about female inmates before. They were tired, and we settled them down. I went home very late that night.

For the next several weeks I worked at least two shifts per day. Some institutions sent over what female officers they had. There was a special emergency hiring set in place. It would be boring to read all of the adjustments we had to make, but certainly having men and women together was a challenge, to say the least. The best control we had was to let the men know that any slight infraction would result in an immediate transfer to another institution. We did not have that type of leverage with the women. Surprisingly, this togetherness caused many of the men to clean up. There was less cursing. Many started to dress to impress.

The women settled in with major complaints. One day, I went to the female housing unit to have a meeting. It was there I learned how many more issues were involved with women. There were physical ailments and conditions the men did not have. There were items needed by women that men did not need. There were more concerns for the children. There were pregnant inmates being brought in by sheriff departments. Some used children as an excuse for trying to obtain more privileges. At that meeting, one woman went out of control about her children. I did not handle myself well at all. Control center was listening over the intercom system. Officers were sent to the housing unit to stop a brawl. The Boss later had a talk with me about how I must control myself when meeting with them. This was another case of men working better with women, and women being able to control the actions of the men better.

When I first started at MSP, male officers felt female officers could not do the same job; however, what men did with physical prowess, we females did with our instincts and behavior toward the male offenders. Many times the female way of handling a situation was far more beneficial, and without the use of force. When the Boss talked to the female inmates, he had a totally calming effect on them. I did not, especially in the beginning. The women thought they could "con" a man quicker than they could another female. I think this is true in most cases.

There are exceptions to all rules. If a staff member was weak, brought family situations or a midlife crisis to work, or just was vulnerable to the opposite sex, inmates would use these weakness for their own purposes. If the staff member became too involved, some "snitch" would tell on them. The employee was usually terminated. Some of these situations had an adverse effect on the inmate also.

We continued to grow and learn. New programs were added and staff hired. It was difficult to find jobs for the women and still keep the sexes separated. Games were beginning to be played. We found out early we could not have men and women in church services together. We confiscated a sweat suit from a woman who had sewed a small zipper in the bottom of the suit. Romances started from afar and notes were passed. All officers had to be on their toes. We fed the women separately in the dining hall. Visiting privileges had to be monitored closely. We obtained more volunteers to help with the women's issues. Somehow we all adjusted and settled into our new situation. Conduct violations for men were reduced to almost nothing. They all wanted to stay at RCC (I wonder why). Many male inmates from other institutions requested to come to our co-correctional institution. All was good.

In 1976, RCC changed again. All women were transferred from the women's institution in Tipton to RCC. All men were moved out, except for a cadre of fifty for maintenance and some farm work. Eventually the farming operation was to be phased out. Again our population of inmates flip-flopped, but we were still co-corrections. This is where the story really begins for RCC.

In 1976, I (along with many others) was given a plaque for outstanding service to the Department of Corrections. This plaque was presented to me by Missouri Governor Christopher "Kit" Bond at the Capitol. He later became a senator in Washington, DC. It was a great honor. My son was allowed to attend and walk with me to receive the plaque. It was during the time I was an identification and records officer. I was nominated by the Boss.

More emphasis was being placed on female inmates in the department. One reason was their numbers were increasing by leaps and bounds. The new sentence of fifty years without parole for inmates convicted of murder was being given to females as well as males. They were referred to as "fifty-year stips." We now had three levels of security: maximum, medium, and minimum.

We had to change rules, secure the fence and front gate, make a reception center for women, and increase our medical services. We built an administrative segregation unit referred to by both staff and inmates as "the hole." There was one in every institution. It could be used as a holding area, or an inmate might be assigned to that unit temporarily. Several female inmates made the segregation unit their home. We had nowhere to transfer the problem inmates. We constructed a series of single cells in the basement of the administration building, which was dark and a bit musty. Our psychologist was before his time with color therapy—the cells were painted calming colors. I was told the officers called it "Motel 6" with a pink room, although I can't verify this. Bad things did happen down there. Officers were treated badly by certain inmates. At any moment, feces or urine could be thrown at them. It happened many times. The officers could be grabbed if they were not security minded.

During this period, the men took a backseat but seemed happy just to be in co-corrections. There were many interesting stories about the women.

One of the first new women I met was a big, tall woman who came up to me and said, "You know, I am a homosexual." Her reputation had preceded her. She was a long-term inmate who preyed on young women. I responded, "Yes, I do know. It's none of my business. However, if you force another inmate to accept your preference, it then becomes my business." I think my answer shocked her. She seemed to be disappointed she didn't get the reaction she had hoped for. She didn't bother me again. I didn't like this woman, because she was indeed a predator.

I read the file of a woman who was convicted of rape because she assisted a man in a rape of another woman. She also had mental health issues and allegedly ate frogs. I met this woman. We got to know each other. We respected each other. She had a history of violence in the former institution. She came up one day (she was as tall as I was) and asked what I would do if she started a fight with me. I bravely told her, "You would not be standing." She actually believed that. We laughed together. I do believe it was a serious question. Before she was transferred, she left me a picture of her and signed it. She became a big problem in another institution, though.

There were two young ladies I'll never forget. One was a young German woman who had been brought to the United States knowing not one word of English. She was thrown into a classroom without the benefit of language training. She began acting out at an early age, and continued her bad behavior even after she came to RCC. She would fight a male or female officer and sometimes would win for a moment. She was placed in segregation in a single cell, with shackles on wrists and legs. Later an officer found she had knocked the toilet stool out of the outside wall. She was looking outside, laughing at the staff. This was a small woman. She never totally adjusted but did respect the Boss, me, and some other staff members. She once kissed my cheek during a program. Actually, the Boss told her to go over and kiss me. He would do things like that and laugh his head off. His laughter sounded through the institution always. I was told she left RCC, married, and was doing well.

The other woman was a tall, thin woman with sickle cell anemia. The disease did not stop her from being very dangerous. She came in with a three-year sentence and was released approximately twenty years later. She kept piling on years to serve because she had assaulted so many officers. She remained in administrative segregation during her stay at RCC. She injured two female officers by knocking them down; they fell on the concrete floor. She was put in total isolation because she disturbed all of the inmates in the area. She had no friends at all. Her wrists were so small she could easily slip out of handcuffs.

One day a male officer opened the isolation door to bring her out. He walked in with a shield. She flew over the shield, bit him, and knocked him down. She would never be rehabilitated. She was in prison when her only son died in another prison. I wonder if she is living today.

Another woman either had mental health problems or was a good actress. She remained naked all the time, even during that special time of the month. She was eventually released and was reportedly doing well.

That is segregation in a female institution. You and I cannot imagine what happens in a male institution. RCC did try to make this a better place, but it was necessary to segregate problem inmates. One year there was a sunrise service in the unit. A chaplain gave the ceremony. Several staff, including me, attended. It was very impressive and appreciated by most.

There were so many women I met who left impressions on me. Many were the female officers. They all moved up through the ranks at RCC thanks to the Boss. He believed in promoting women and also in treating female inmates with respect. Most women—staff and inmates—respected the Boss. He was normally a gentle man but could stand his ground with anyone. The only female inmate I know he had troubles with is the one I mentioned above. My office was next to his. One day that inmate was in the office with the Boss and an officer. I heard a loud thump on the wall. I raced in to see if help was needed. The inmate had come over the desk at him. He knocked her against the wall. She did not file suit and settled down for a while.

When RCC received all of the females, we had to develop a reception center much like an entire institution used for the men. The men's diagnostic center was called the Reception and Diagnostic Center. It was located in a nearby town. This institution was built because MSP could not hold all new receptions. I learned how to fingerprint. I had to fingerprint every woman who came in from sheriff departments from all over the state. I was treated for scabies once due to handling the inmate' hands; however, it turned out to be an allergy. The thought made me feel dirty. The reception center was a housing unit in the basement at the front of the institution, where many of the administrative offices had now been located. During this time, my position was upgraded to a record officer II. The only other record officer II was a male at the reception center for men. Later more positions became available, but I was the first female record officer II. It put me in a supervisory position, which made me more eligible for promotion. This was another milestone for me. The additional money helped with the raising of my son.

Reception was interesting. One woman was brought in from a sheriff's department on a gurney with an IV in her arm. She was having a miscarriage. The sheriff did not want the expense of medical costs. RCC had to send her to the medical center at the University of Missouri-Columbia, where we sent many of our sick inmates. Officers had to observe the inmates around the clock while they were in the hospital. Pregnant women had their babies there. They could keep the baby if the family would assume responsibility for it. If not, the baby would be put up for adoption. RCC had a close call. The court had decided that one inmate would be able to keep her baby at our institution. The staff and the Boss were in a frenzy. There was a medical reason for this, said the court. We were preparing a tiny room, which was attached to our small visiting room with access to a bathroom. The woman and her baby would have to have officer coverage around the clock. We could not place her in a dormitory because of liability for the baby. Shortly before she was to be brought to RCC, the court gave her parole. What a relief.

Another interesting decision was made regarding our reception center. The first transvestite came into the male reception center. The person was in the middle of a sex change and was on female hormones. No one in the department knew what to do with the inmate. Guess which institution he was sent to? RCC, of course, was the institution the inmate was sent to. This is actually a compliment to RCC—it meant we could handle almost any situation.

This person had both a male and female name. When the inmate came to the institution, the Boss was his usual creative self with his plan to handle the situation. First, one of our female sergeants had to strip search the person. The sergeant came out of the room with a strong blush on her face. She said the person had male parts but they were tied up. The person appeared effeminate but still looked male. Permission was given to continue the hormones. The inmate was placed in reception in a private cell. He remained there with privileges until his release. Please remember, this inmate was in a female reception center. During the time the inmate was there, this person apparently stopped taking hormones. The inmate took on a male appearance including a beard and a drop in his tone of voice. Can anyone imagine in this day and time what lawsuits would come from the families and the female inmates in reception? No suits were filed. After the person left, it was rumored that AIDS contributed to his/her death. The gossip chain for inmates, in or out, is usually true. As I said earlier, I learned in this career more than some people could imagine in a lifetime.

During this time, an affirmation action committee was formed, with the Boss as the first president. There were subsequent presidents; I served one year. It was good at that time and appeared to be sanctioned by the department. It was needed during the early years of integrating more female and black staff members into DOC. The committee dissolved when women and blacks started receiving better pay and promotions, and the hiring increased.

As I said before, our Boss was more progressive than corrections in general. Our staff was 100 percent behind him. If he had a new idea, we would all brainstorm. If we had an idea, he would listen. The idea was perfected with coordinated efforts. We became a very progressive, unusual institution. Some staff at other institutions had a few laughs at our expense, but RCC did not care. For example, one perfect summer day, the Boss rounded up all eligible female inmates and took them on an excursion to the river. It was not far away. We obtained fishing poles and bait. Many inmates had never fished before. It was a day of great outdoor activities. They were all tired and slept well that night. It also gave others an incentive to do better.

Several female staff had developed an activity around Christmastime. We would select four of the most difficult inmates for a trip to see the Christmas lights. They would be placed on "out count" to us, which meant we were responsible for them. Any time inmates left the institution, an out count was prepared, which included the list of inmates, their pictures, and our signatures. After the Christmas lights, they were taken to one of our homes to see the tree and have lots of candy. They became normal people again. When they came back to the institution, their behavior changed 90 percent for the better. Again, it was an incentive for others. Courts, potential lawsuits, policy, and general procedures would not permit this activity today. I'll be the first to say it could have backfired on us, but we did it, and it didn't.

I refer to people in prison as "inmates," because that is the name I used the most. When I first started in DOC, they were either "convicts" or "prisoners." The terms changed over the years, depending on the mood of the government. For a while, there was a mandate in DOC to call the inmates "residents"— someone thought it was a more respectful name. I was in a meeting with male inmates at RCC, and I referred to them as "residents," as I had been told. One guy called me on it. He did not like it at all. He said, "A resident is someone who wants to be here. I do not." I asked him what he would prefer to be called. He said, "Call us 'convicts.' That's what we are." In my later years, I worked with probationers. They are called "clients." This change has been difficult for me. The word "offender" was also a popular name during part of the history.

A good part of my book recalls particular cases and inmates. There were so many unique people and situations in this world I worked in. I was never bored. I loved almost every day I came to work. How many people can say that? Despite the trauma, the discrimination, the hard work, all the crazy things, it was never dull. My adrenaline kept pumping. On my own, I slowly learned to profile, which was a wonderful tool I lived by. I became very good at it. It worked well for me in prisons, but in my personal life, it could really get me into trouble. I do it with everyone I meet. It makes me look negative to many people and can ruin a friendship. I would say, however, I am usually 80 percent right in my profiles.

In profiling, the thing you must look at the most is the childhood. This is the key to why people are what and who they are. Changing the lessons learned in childhood works better with younger inmates. The older ones resist any change of behavior and are more challenging. Does everyone change or become rehabilitated? No. We can only do the best we can. We hope to change at least one aspect of their thinking or their life. If you want more, you will soon be disappointed and give up. I guess my gift is one of the reasons I love the show *Criminal Minds*. I am definitely not that good, but I give it my best shot.

Another thing the reader might be thinking–what about women and men living together? I would ask you to think about any situation where men and women are in close proximity. Did we have pregnancies at RCC? Yes, we did. There were five documented pregnancies during ten years of co-corrections. I am sure there were more. I think that's a pretty good record actually. Was there mingling of staff and inmates of the opposite sex? There was with consequence.

The department made a policy about this issue later. It was negative for staff, because they were usually terminated. With the new policy, they could also be prosecuted. The inmate got no punishment, because the belief was that the inmates were captives of the staff. This made staff responsible. Many of these women and men were master manipulators; not all staff could resist the manipulation. I told one male inmate he could manipulate me only as far as I wanted to be manipulated. Manipulation was a game played by both staff and inmates. I almost always knew what was happening but I would sometimes let it go to get the real story. Some staff used "snitches" and then made promises that were legally hard to keep. An inmate never gives up information without a reason. I always told them I would not promise anything but I wanted to hear what they had to say. I usually got the information I wanted because the inmates liked to tell.

I have read extreme Christian views about the treatment of inmates in prison. I will definitely tell you that some of the outside volunteers who became involved with inmates were members of the clergy. An inmate told on a member of the clergy. When the minister was asked about the sexual overtures, he said he was trying to make the inmate understand the work of God. Another clergyman was heavily involved with female inmates. I do not know if there was physical contact. He made the staff miserable with his requests for these certain women. He was later defrocked. I was actually glad because I knew how the inmates manipulated him and he fell for it.

The institution was asked by KPLR-TV (January 1980) to bring female inmates to St. Louis for a panel discussion on Phone Power. There were call-ins with questions for the panel. There was a late night soap opera on KPLR called *Prisoner Cell Block H*. It was a soap opera about female inmates. I watched it myself and laughed. I was chosen, along with another female staff member, to take the women to the television station, and I also participated in the panel. It went well. I was thrilled to be a part of a TV panel.

I asked for a male officer to accompany us because I was no longer in the custody force, and the inmates were high security. The TV station was in a less safe part of St. Louis. Even though our Boss did not tolerate any discrimination toward inmates or staff, there was always at least one male staff member who could be described as a "macho" man. The captain in charge of assigning an officer to accompany us said to me, "JoAnn, if you get raped, maybe you will smile more often." Oh, why did I not file a suit?

Ironically, later, when the Boss was away, I was in charge of the institution. This captain, who carried a state-issued gun, was home one day, drinking. He was also having family problems. He called the institution threatening to kill himself with a state-issued gun. Oh, the press.... I had no training to deal with a situation like this, but I got on the phone and talked to him until our staff psychologist arrived at the captain's home forty-five minutes later.

This was a man I disliked, but I managed to put the feelings aside in hopes he would not commit suicide. The psychologist got there and the man gave the gun up. Talk about stressful. He later married a former female inmate. He no longer had a career with DOC. At this point, I will add it has been proved that some corrections staff (particularly officers) are subject to have family problems, divorces, alcohol problems, and some were known to be sadistic. The environment they work in daily could breed these negative issues.

In July 1978, the Boss needed official help with his administrative duties. He felt some of us should get credit for what we were doing, if not pay. He appointed four of us to acting positions—two men and two women. My duties were to supervise the record office, legal services, personnel, planning operations, staff training including volunteers, human relations, and mail room. This not only took a burden off the superintendent but it gave us supervisory experience on paper. We had already been doing much of this from the beginning. These appointments led to the department creating superintendent I, II, and III positions for all institutions. The title "warden" would remain at MSP until much later in DOC history. In 2012, there are now deputy wardens and wardens in each institution. Now I consider myself a former deputy warden, and I like that title.

In 1981, another change came to our little institution. Due to overcrowding of the female population, a minimum-security institution for men in Chillicothe, Missouri, was turned into a minimum-security institution for women. That left RCC with maximum and medium-security women and minimum-security men. The department was constantly making changes, and we all just rolled with those changes. Having this new institution gave the women an incentive for good behavior. If their custody was reduced to minimum, they would be sent to the new institution.

It was during this time that the director (former warden of MSP) called the Boss and me to his office. He offered me the superintendent position at Chillicothe. No one is alive who can verify this, and I'm sure he told no one else. I declined. He said the Boss and I would receive a pay raise. When the time came, the Boss got a raise and I did not. I was told there was no money for me.

Sometime in the eighties, the Boss went to California to see a new program call MATCH (Mothers and Their Children). He came back excited. Staff and volunteers put their heads together and developed a program called PATCH (Parents and their Children). The institution could not staff it, so volunteers from many churches took over. The institution was given a trailer. RCC managed to put a fence around it and we had a program. PATCH was the first of its kind in Missouri and probably in the Midwest. MATCH officials helped us with the setup. The trailer was furnished like a house with various beds for children.

Mothers and fathers were able to visit with their children in a homelike setting with volunteer supervision. This was a high privilege. Inmates had to earn their way to the trailer. Sometimes two volunteers supervised a husband, wife, and children, but that was not the norm. Later, PATCH programs were started in other institutions. The parent was allowed to read a book to the child and an audio of the parent was given to the child. This is now being done in many institutions, but our little RCC was one of the first. It was a great step toward maintaining family ties, which contributed to reducing the recidivism rate (the percentage of offenders coming back to prison). The volunteers were such an asset to our institution.

PRISON
PATCH®
PARENTS AND THEIR CHILDREN

Our Mission Is
To Strengthen and Maintain Family
Relationships During Parental Incarcerations.

Nothing has been said about women convicted of murder or those who had the sentence of fifty years without parole. There were many. Equality for women in America was advancing. With that, equality in sentencing was also more prominent. Many of these women were not allowed to bring domestic violence evidence into the courtroom, which is now acceptable under certain circumstances. I came to know these inmates personally. I appreciated the feelings about the long sentences; however, I did not agree everyone had a domestic violence defense. Many of these women knew exactly what they were doing, in some cases committing premeditated murder. One woman married a man connected to the Mafia and had a child with him. I didn't know all of the circumstances but I do know her plan for his murder was carefully thought-out. She hired someone to kill her husband. After serving several years, she was given her freedom because of the influential people who surrounded her. I did not agree with her release, but I just did my job.

I knew another female inmate who hated her husband. I'm sure there were some abuse issues. She decided to run over him with a car, but instead of running over him, she ran over another man who was standing beside him. I tried not to smile but I couldn't help it. She began to laugh also, because it had been several years. How would it feel to be sentenced to fifty years without parole for killing the wrong man? Unbelievable, but she committed murder, and the court did not care.

These stories go on and on. Another woman convinced her son to kill one of her husbands. She received fifty years without parole; he got life in prison. She has since been released after serving many years. One elderly woman, not at our institution, received the death penalty because her husband forced her to help him commit several grisly murders. She helped bury the bodies in their backyard. Finally she was given life. There was a woman from another culture who received the death penalty. She and her husband killed their daughter because the daughter was promiscuous and in their culture, that was the punishment. She was never put to death.

I would like to inject a word of well-learned wisdom for volunteers and people just starting in the criminal justice system as staff. DO NOT THINK YOU ARE THE SAVIORS OF THE INMATES YOU SERVE. You make a difference in their lives, but do not expect too much. You will burn out and be no good to anyone.

This story is a case in point. Early on when the women first came to RCC, a young, extremely overweight woman came into reception. She was toothless and a hard-core drug abuser. Yet she had a college degree, and she was from an affluent section of St. Louis County. It appeared she had everything a young woman could have. After she was processed and cleared, she was assigned as our cleaner. I will call her "JB." JB won the hearts of all working in that administrative section. We were certain that with our help she would be rehabilitated. We made sure she got false teeth. We helped her lose weight. We thought we built up her self-esteem. She was a model inmate in every way.

On the day she was released, JB asked me if she could stop by my house. I had to tell her no. It was against the rules. Less than a year after she left, we got word (through the inmate grapevine) she had been found shot in the drug-infested ghetto of St. Louis City. A drug deal had gone bad. Apparently the skin was worn off her hands because she had tried to push herself up off the pavement. She was in a coma and died shortly thereafter. I took this home with me. I had nightmares of seeing her lying on that dirty street. She was on my mind constantly. I felt I had let her down by not allowing her to contact me.

Our wonderful psychologist was a listening ear for staff also. He said we should write a letter of condolence to her mother. We did just that. A letter came and the contents were as cold as ice. She thanked us graciously, but throughout the whole letter, you could almost feel that the mother was grateful JB was dead. Remember me telling you about family influence? She had material things but not the love or support of her mother. I learned another very important lesson. Whatever happens, I leave it when I walk out the gate or door. I shared this experience with volunteers lately, but I'm not sure I got through to them.

Another female inmate I must tell about. She was in our institution twice. The first time, she became sickly, and she went back and forth to the medical center in Columbia. She was released. When she came back on another charge, she was even sicker. She had been out quite some time. She began to tell other inmates she had cancer to receive pity. She wanted their sympathy and for those so inclined, she wanted a sexual relationship. One young woman became very fond of her. Later in her stay, she was diagnosed with HIV. She was the first person I ever knew who actually was given the diagnosis. It was very scary for all of us because she had been sick for years before the official diagnosis. The Boss insisted she get together with those inmates with whom she'd had a physical relationship and tell them the truth. At that time, there was no prodical for HIV/AIDS.

She was later released and again, through the grapevine, we learned that she died. This made one feel it was possible to survive for several years even with no known medical treatment. A question is how many people she infected. She could have infected other women in and out of the corrections system. In the prison system, HIV became a serious, dangerous subject for staff and inmates. Staff had to wear very thick gloves for housing unit searches due to the possibility of needle pricks. No one really knew how the disease was passed. Spit, blood, and bites were things to avoid.

I must say a bit about the person who stabbed the superintendent of the female institution in 1976. We will call her "Sam." She was a small person and did her time well; however, this was the one inmate I would never trust or turn my back on. When I looked at her, I recalled the brutal stabbing and could never forget it. She served a long sentence and was later transferred. I have not heard what happened to her. Several female inmates with life or fifty years have now been released by a governor. I worked with many of them for over ten years. After my retirement I wrote a letter to the governor of Missouri for one of these women. Immediately after I mailed the letter, the governor was killed in a plane crash, but she was released several years later by another governor. She had not one conduct violation on her record. It disappointed me when she talked badly about the prison system after she was released. She was treated very well, considering she was an inmate with a long sentence.

During the years after 1974, the mood of the nation became one of emphasis on programming. It varied from governor to governor and from president to president: either lock them up and throw away the key or give them programs. Everyone had their finger in the pie for programs. RCC, as I already mentioned, was very innovative and progressive. As the money came, so did the programs. Our education program flourished. All inmates under the age of twenty-one were required to be in a GED program, and the others were strongly encouraged. Early on, with only male inmates, we sent a chosen few to Lincoln University (historically black college) and they received college degrees. Several were very successful in life. A program at a dormitory on the University of Missouri-Rolla campus was not so successful. Lack of supervision was a problem and the program folded. When the dormitory was cleaned out, drugs, knives, and other contraband were found. It was a good idea but not close enough for RCC to supervise properly.

RCC added a data entry program which did work for many state agencies. It was a very good experience to leave the institution with. Quick Print was also established under the director of Missouri Correctional Enterprises. It did well and was profitable. An auto mechanics class was started but it only lasted approximately nine months. The information systems program was very successful. Inmates learned to become computer programmers, which provided excellent skills for when they were released. In addition to the parenting program

I've discussed, RCC also offered ongoing parenting classes and prenatal classes. Yes, there were several pregnant inmates at RCC, as I stated earlier. Drug classes and twelve step programs were run by volunteers. Later a substance abuse counselor was placed in every institution.

During these years, RCC had to be totally evacuated several times due to flooding, and we were on standby with buses waiting outside the compound more times than I can remember. The Missouri River was a force to reckon with. RCC staff and inmates could be ready to evacuate with little notice. The procedure was in place. Everyone knew their duties. We did have help from many other institutions. MSP sent their emergency squad to help us. Their guns made me very nervous, as they did the inmates; there was no real need, since at times like this, the inmates were very compliant. We never had an escape during flood time.

We did, of course, have our share of escapes, as did the other institutions. During one of the female escapes, the Boss and one of our directors were out looking for her. They got word that she was in a local store. The Boss went into the store and successfully apprehended her with his official badge (he thought). It turned out he produced his NAACP card. That was not easily forgotten. We all got a big laugh out of it.

RENZ CORRECTIONAL CENTER

1982–1990

The year of 1982 was a real milestone in my life. RCC was given a superintendent I position as an assistant to the Boss. Missouri had a merit system for most state employees. Anyone wanting a state position or promotion competed with a written test combined with experience/education. I made a good written score. Many of the male staff had far more experience than any of the women, and none of us could make a score high enough to compete with the men. The Boss insisted the merit system give RCC a register of names of only female employees for his and the committee's consideration. He said a female *would be* in a high position in an institution which housed maximum security women. In August 1982, I was promoted to superintendent I. I was elated (little did I know what was later in store). I was, I believe, the first female assistant superintendent in the department. There were rumors going around that I did not deserve this promotion because I'd just piggybacked on the Boss's success, but I didn't care. I knew I worked hard to deserve the promotion. I didn't care what anyone might think.

Assistant Superintendent Badge

The Boss did make promotions possible for me, other women, and blacks, but I know without a doubt that I carried my weight. I was blessed with a knack for this type of work. During this turbulent time of integrating more women and minorities into the Department of Corrections, the DOC had developed basic and advanced training. The training center developed a class specifically addressing the role of female officers working in institutions. I was asked, along with a female officer, to develop and teach a class. It was very rewarding for me but it did meet with some resistance from the male trainees. This did not bother me at all, because I was used to resistance. The class was held for a few years until it was decided there was no longer a need.

My son also graduated from high school in 1982. He had a difficult time growing up because of my working in corrections— he grew up around inmates and the officer mentality of his mother. I was a strict parent and probably almost a father figure.

His grandmother took on more of the mother role. I was able to participate in most of his activities. He brought his rock band to RCC to perform. The women loved it. He also did his Eagle Scout project there. He had a clothing drive for the inmates of RCC. He and I saw Chuck Berry at RCC. It was interesting to say the least. The Boss and his band backed Berry.

He was a good student but had some behavioral problems. I didn't miss much of his behavior, and my gut served us well in raising him. Sometimes I believe I was a bit harsh—I remember telling him I would rather shoot him than see him behind those walls. After graduation, he went on to accomplish great things which I will discuss at the end of the book. It took stress off me to know he made it through his teen years. Corrections was becoming extremely complicated, and my leadership role took up quite a bit of my time. As one of the supervisors, I had to take duty every six weeks, which meant carrying a pager and being available for any emergency or situation at my institution during nights/weekends. I couldn't really plan anything. I also took much of the Boss's weekend duty in the evenings because he was playing in a band.

I have spent a lot of time in this book telling you about issues from 1976 on because it was a turbulent period in all of our lives. Co-corrections for Missouri did gain quite a bit of publicity, and the Missouri Legislature finally decided it had gone on long enough. Men and women had to be separated. In 1986, all female inmates were moved to Chillicothe and to Fulton Diagnostic and Reception Center. RCC again became an all-male minimum-security institution. Again staff had to adapt and change the whole picture of the institution.

The men who came were only used to a minority of female staff at their prior institutions. At RCC, the female staff members were the majority. The men had the mistaken idea they could charm the female staff. It didn't happen. RCC had very strong female staff members who knew their jobs and were not afraid to do them. After a while, when a female officer asked a male inmate to raise his arms for a pat search, he asked, "How high?" Female officers were permitted to do this type of search. In an emergency, if no male staff was available, two female officers were permitted to strip search one male inmate, although this situation was very rare.

At that time, many citizens had very strange, degrading ideas of working in a prison, particularly about women who worked in a prison. I went to a church function to speak about our parenting program. During the discussion, a woman told me she thought any female corrections officer was a prostitute; several others agreed with her. I tried to dispel the myth, but I'm not sure I was successful. Even my family at one time said women should not be working as officers at a male prison. I quickly said that if it were not for that job when my son was small, I would have been on assistance. You cannot support yourself and a family on a clerk's salary. I am proud of the decision I made. It was the best decision for my family.

RCC again settled in, and the staff and the inmates adjusted. There was a female lieutenant who observed better than anyone I ever knew. An inmate was walking out of the dining hall, and the lieutenant pulled him over for a search. She found quite a bit of stolen food. The inmate asked the lieutenant how she knew. She said, "Because you spoke to me, and you never do." Just that small variation in behavior made the difference. We were trained to spot these changes. One example of my ability to observe was personal and in a grocery store, where I was cashing a check. I could feel something happening in the store. I told the worker to call the police because there was an incident, but she thought I had lost my mind. A group of young men ran out of the store with liquor. I was left standing and waiting on my money.

Another incident I recall happened in a grocery store in Virginia after I retired. A man came up to me pretending he knew me from a landscaping service. He wanted money because his wife, he said, was stranded on an interstate. I walked off to the other side of the store. I found a young manager, and I told him there was a scam artist in the store. I even pointed the man out. The manager took no action and had no clue. Later I read in the local paper that this person had scammed several people and a church. I called local authorities. Nothing was done. Later, another paper from the Hampton Roads area stated this man was moving everywhere, but the article claimed there was no description of him. This made me angry, so I called the crime line again, and I told them—again—what I knew. I gave a complete description of him. I have no idea if the person was caught or moved on.

We kept the same programs and staff after the women left. Minimum-security men do have fewer behavioral problems. Boredom set in. My need for the adrenaline high was great. The Boss laid back some, because he was starting to think about retirement. I thought about finding something exciting or different to do. A female staff member, who was in charge of inmate activities, and I developed a plan—a good plan. The program "Scared Straight" was much publicized at that time, but we did not want a harsh program, and in the opinions of today's criminal justice planners, it was not the thing to do. We started a program called "Reaching Out." One man even designed a T-shirt with a chained hand holding children and an inmate as if reaching out. It was great and said it all.

Reaching Out T-Shirt

My duties as superintendent I in a small institution were different from duties in larger institutions. The Boss made the overall decisions and completed the executive duties. I supervised all the sections of the instruction, including personnel, records, classification, maintenance, food service, custody, and many small sections. There were programs in our institution run by other DOC departments, but RCC still had the final say. Even with that long list of responsibilities, I became restless and wanted to do more. Reaching Out became my project, with the help of the institutional activities coordinator. A long-term inmate wanted to start a similar program, but with his own ideas and rules. He had some good ideas but they had to be modified. This wasn't going to work.

Inmates submitted applications. Their record at RCC had to be totally clean, with no conduct violations or "write- ups." We handpicked a group: black and white, young and older, with varied backgrounds. We selected two blacks and two whites to be inmate moderators. They had strict guidelines, and we supervised every program. The moderators guided the group in all ways, with us watching. Normally the group setting was a circle, with one inmate beside one child.

The group bloomed. We became known at many juvenile institutions and schools, and we also incorporated girls in the group. Requests and commendations came pouring in; some are documented. There was no strong-arming, getting in the juveniles' faces, curse words, etc. other than rarely, to prove a point. For example: the male juveniles were given a description of the male reception center. The inmates had their favorite jargon to tell these boys that if they came in they would be used by older inmates. "You have choice—you can fight, f…, or climb a tree," they'd say. "Guess what, there are no trees."

Occasionally, a parent would request that their child be allowed to come to the program. Sometimes the juveniles were taken to administrative segregation (the hole) so they could see what detention was all about. Some even asked to be placed in a cell.

The institution received numerous letters complimenting the program. We tried to start a program at the local high school. The school gave us one chance. We presented a panel of inmates during study hall. The first session was sparse, but by the third study hall period, the classroom was packed, because word spread quickly through the school. The teenagers had many questions. It was obvious several had experience with drugs. The inmates would call them on everything. The program was a huge success; however, we were not permitted back. I think the school officials feared retaliation from parents.

LOVE CAN MAKE THE Difference

HERE WE All sit in this great Big circle
For which we must All give thanks
To MRS schupp AND MRS MerTeNS
For giving us the Opportunity To TEll our stories
About the HARD Times in our lives
which were filled, with pain and no glory
But we Now have A chance
To give of ourselves
something that some day
could help someone else
And if WE CAN oNly save
ONE person out of tEN
WE would then have to chalk it up
As A very big wiN
And Hope ANd Pray, THAt the other NiNE
CAN keep there selves in line
So that they woN't NEVEr, HAVE to come iN HERE
And do some HARd Time.

Poem by an unknown inmate at RCC.

We had so many inmate applications, we could not possibly accept them all until a member was released or left the program. The inmate who tried very hard to run the program finally came around to our thinking and was as proud as the rest. We also decided to teach these male inmates how to have fun without drugs or crime. We had barbecues at the trailer beyond the institution and brought our families. Everyone had a ball. We had to caution the group not to become arrogant with the rest of the inmates. They didn't do that, to my knowledge, although they did have the idea they were special.

Our purpose in creating this group was to help juveniles, but more and more, as we met with the inmates and saw them with the juveniles, we knew it was also helping them. The group became very close-knit. They watched each other's behavior at the institution. A very good example is a young man I will call Mic. He had drug problems and came in with a bad attitude; he had beaten someone. Mic took to the Reaching Out group and really got into it. A group of male and female juveniles came to our circle. During the discussion, a young woman said, "None of you can help me, because I have been sexually abused." There was a long silence with our inmates. Most men do not readily make it known if they have been abused, especially in a prison setting, because it makes them very vulnerable.

Suddenly, Mic said, "I can help you." He told the group that he had been placed with his brothers in a foster home for a while. The parents came back to get his brothers but left him. During that time in the foster home, some male sexually abused him several times. When he finally got out on his own, he began acting out. Mic had lots of anger issues, which led him to a life of crime and prison. He talked with the girl for quite some time, but he finally broke down. We had to remove him from group. After that time, Mic became a model inmate, and it was a joy to watch him grow. As I've said, the family, or lack thereof, has much to do with what happens when a child grows up.

This is when I finally realized the respect within the group. Inmates tell. No question about it. The inmates in this group were asked not to reveal Mic's secret because it would be the talk of the institution, and it could put him in harm's way. Not one word came out of the group about Mic's sexual abuse. In fact, we monitored several inmates and Mic in a group session to allow him to talk about it more. At his request, not all members of the group were asked to attend. It seemed to help him to share with the group.

Before Mic was released from the institution, he and I talked. He still had the question of why his parents did not come back for him. I told him, if he could, to try to see them and ask them that question, but that he needed to be prepared to get an answer that might upset him. I also talked to him about young women and his relationships with them. When he was released, he went to Arizona to talk with his parents. They did not give him the answers he wanted, but he did have an answer. Much later, he sent a letter with a picture to me at RCC. The picture was of him, his wife, and a beautiful baby boy. He said he listened to me about relationships. He thought he had picked a woman I would approve of. I have not heard from Mic since but I believe he has made a good life for himself. This is what we hope will happen, but it is not always so.

I received a card from the grandmother of one of the group members. It was hardly legible, because she was eighty-four years old. She thanked me for my kindness to her grandson. I still cherish the card. This man also seemed to flourish. We tried to keep track as best we could after they were released. Usually, if they were doing well, we heard nothing. One of our moderators was released and later came back into the penal system with a sex charge. This was unreal to us. He was a great speaker, and the juveniles listened to him; he seemed to have his life together. Another moderator from the group left RCC, came back to DOC several times, and later was killed as an indirect result of continued drug abuse. He just could not kick the habit. Remember the NA slogan—jails, institutions, or death.

Another man in the group (Terry) wanted a furlough to see his family. A furlough was written permission to leave the institution for a period of time to go to a specific place—it was quite a privilege. The inmate had to be screened very carefully. I talked to him for quite some time. I told him his record was not good, and I feared he might not come back. He begged me to submit the papers. I made him promise to come back, and I told him that I personally would come after him if he didn't. He again promised he would come back. I talked to the Boss, who gave his permission with reluctance. The man went home and came back. He was happy and very appreciative. Later, he was transferred to another institution. He was given a furlough there, possibly because he had one successful furlough under his belt, and he never returned. Do I think I made the right decision, or did I set him up for failure? I don't know, and I never will. I trusted his word, and it paid off. I also feel he respected me enough to not want to let me down. I never heard what happened to him later.

I cannot stress enough that women must learn to gain the respect of male inmates when working with them. I saw many good female workers come and go, by falling in love with a male inmate. In most cases, the female staff member was fired, and the inmate went on with his life. The likelihood of a lasting relationship was very small. The chance of the inmate telling someone about the situation was great. It was the same for male staff and female inmates.

I will cite two incidents of respect I observed when working with the male offenders. One involved me. At one time, it was my responsibility to approve all requests for work release outside the institution. I denied a young man because the file indicated he was not a good candidate. That day I took a walk outside the fence of the institution at lunch hour, as I usually did. As I walked, I heard a voice from the housing units say, "Ms. Mertens, you old bitch." I knew it was the voice of the young man whom I turned down earlier. I couldn't prove this; thus, I couldn't write a conduct violation. I was angry, of course, but that's life in an institution.

Later that afternoon, the day lieutenant came into my office laughing. He said, "Guess who checked into protective custody? Protective custody is total lockdown. Inmates are placed there, usually by request, if they fear living in the general population for some reason. The inmate was the young man who called me the name. As you might imagine, the men who respected me threatened him for saying that, so then he wanted protection. Is this a correct means of justice? No. It is life within a prison, and the inmates have unwritten rules. I felt very comfortable with my safety, because I knew my back was covered. I accepted their means of protection. I knew I was respected by the majority of the inmates. Again, fair, firm, and consistent was the key.

Another example of this unwritten rule of respect involved a teacher in a classroom in a more remote area of the school. Officers checked frequently, but for the most part, the teacher handled the classroom. One male inmate became very angry with the teacher. He stood over her desk in a threatening manner. She did not have time to call for assistance. When she looked past the angry man, she saw that the other inmates in the class had circled him to protect her. He backed off and was removed by custody staff from the classroom. This teacher was highly respected by the inmates.

From 1986 to 1989, RCC was a very relaxed, minimum-security institution. The Boss was thinking more and more of retirement. I was thinking of moving up the ladder. Working conditions were now good in the Missouri Department of Corrections. The female population in DOC was increasing by leaps and bounds. Judges were more likely to sentence women as they did the men—with equality of the sexes there also come some unpleasant consequences. This was one of them. In 1989, we got the word—RCC would be receiving all the maximum-security females along with being the female reception center. The men would be transferred to other institutions around the state. The minimum-security females would be housed at Chillicothe, Missouri.

"Not again," the staff and inmates cried. "This is just too much change in a three-year period." With maximum-security females, we would have to shore up security. Actually, few staff really wanted to work with the females because women do have more issues than men, including health problems. The females usually had more connections to their children, more family visits, legal issues involving their children. They just "did time" differently. None of the male inmates wanted to move. A cry came from our Reaching Out group to please place them in good institutions. We tried but could not accommodate all of them.

As usual, our staff made the change in a very successful manner. We were all used to protecting each other, working together for the good of RCC, and preparing to change on short notice. The Boss kept us positive; his laughter had a calming effect on all of us. Once he was eating lunch in our dining room with someone who had a (corrections) radio on. His laughter floated through the airways to all of the institutions.

Again, we were given little time to prepare for this change. After the men moved out, the letters from them poured in to staff. (It was approved for an inmate to write to staff at the institution but never at our homes.) The mail room opened these letters to protect the staff. I received many and have saved them. Two stood out for me. One letter was from the long-timer who had been aggressive about our program. He seemed to have really changed. He expressed his deepest appreciation for being in our program. I hope he did well when he was released. Another card shocked me when I opened it. It said, "To Mom." He apologized for using the term, but he also said that I treated him as a mom should: I corrected him when he was wrong but supported him when he was right. I still cherish that card today. I felt confident I had found the winning combination to working with inmates.

Again the females came. Some we recognized, but there were new ones, too. I was not afraid, as I had been the first time—I knew how to handle the females. Many of the long-timers I had worked with were tied up in appeals of their cases. They were hoping for release soon. The Boss had already made a decision to retire in May of 1990, so this time I worked more closely with the inmates than he did.

I met an unusual female inmate who had the nickname "Heavy Dee." She was stocky and strong. Many people were afraid of her, but she and I hit it off. I asked her one day what was wrong with her neck, because she had scars—or so I thought—in a circle around her neck. She said they were heroin tracks after she shot up so much on the rest of her body. She was very open with me. One time we had to move to Central Missouri Correctional Center briefly because of a flood. The women were housed in the gymnasium. (That story would be a book in itself.) Heavy Dee and I were standing outside smoking (a habit I am now eighteen years free of). A man from one of the male housing unit windows called me an "old bitch," which I brushed off. She was furious with him and told me not to take that. She lifted her finger in a gesture toward him and said, "Yo Mama." I did not hear any response to her words.

These acts of loyalty continued to amaze me during my years in corrections. I did not have to do any illegal favors for the inmates to gain their respect; I just had to treat them with respect. Keep in mind that inmates with severe mental health issues were not to be counted on for anything, but most others could be reasoned with. They liked the sense of honesty. You must show you know the prison culture. It is sometimes hard to understand the thinking of someone so unlike you.

A young woman was brought into the prison. She had eight children with eight different fathers. Her mother was sick with cancer, and she was struggling to take care of those children. I asked the inmate why she kept having children. I discussed tubal ligation with her. She told me she could not do that, because she thought she might get married someday, and if she did, she was sure her husband would want children with her. I had never given this reasoning a thought. The young lady was released but came back shortly thereafter. I called to her when she came in. Her first words were, "Ms. Mertens, at least I'm not pregnant." She had learned something. Small victories are all you can hope for.

RENZ CORRECTIONAL CENTER

1990–1997

In early spring 1990, the *Geraldo* show wanted to tape one of our female inmates who claimed abuse in connection with her crime. Permission was given by central office. I was assigned as the coordinator. It took much planning, so I had telephone contact with the producer often. They were to bring a satellite truck with a crew to the institution, and communication would take place through two separate telephone lines. I was so excited. How would anyone guess I'd be coordinating a TV show in a prison? It was scheduled for May 17, 1990, and right before the show was to be taped, RCC was on flood alert. Because of the threat of flood, the show was moved to Fulton Diagnostic Center. I was needed at RCC, so another staff member took over for me. I was unable to watch the taping or meet the crew.

April 10, 1990

Ms. Jo Ann Mertens
Renz Correctional Center
P.O. Box 28
Cedar City, MO 65022

Dear Jo Ann:

Per our conversations on the phone, I'm putting in writing our formal request to interview Becca   , an inmate at your facility. She was convicted of Capital Murder and is serving a life sentence with no parole.

As you may know, Becca was a battered wife who killed her husband, supposedly, out of self-defense. She was later battered in the justice system, as well, as her judge wouldn't allow any testimony regarding the abuse she withstood within the marriage, and at the county jail, prior to trial. Our focus for this show would be on battered women, and we would very much like to have Becca be a part of it.

Ideally, for us, we would like to tape this show on Thursday, May 10th, at 11 am, Central time. Usually, what works best for you and for us, is if we send a camera crew of two and one producer to your facility and Geraldo stays in New York and does the interview via satellite. This prevents unnecessary chaos, as inmates won't be able to approach Geraldo with their personal stories. Becca would hear the questions through an earpiece and respond to the camera, as our show was actually being taped in our New York studio.

The taping time would take one hour, with probably an extra hour ahead of time to set up. We've worked with correctional departments across the country, and are prepared to cooperate with any of your stipulations and/or concerns.

I'm looking forward to hearing from you, so we can schedule this show. Please call if you have any questions.

Sincerely,

I did watch the show on television and it went well. To not be an actual part of it was a big disappointment to me.

In 1990, an upheaval came into my life and the life of all RCC staff. The Boss was retiring as of May 31, 1990. I had worked with him—or for him—for twenty-four years. He was a leader among leaders. He supported his staff even if they were wrong. He always took the responsibility for his staff's mistakes. I would mention again he was also a saxophone player, singer, and had several bands over the years, and he would continue on with his music and helping seniors after his retirement.

For months, I was waiting for the interview process for this open superintendent II position, which would mean I would finally become an institutional head. This was the dream of my career. During the few years before, the merit system changed how it graded experience and education. The new requirement was a college degree in almost any field. I have seen some strange degrees in the leadership in DOC. My two years in criminal justice would count for nothing in these new specifications. I was upset because I knew it would be used against me. I tried to argue the point with no results. Surely my years of experience should count for something. I scored low on education but high on the written test. All the leaders in DOC knew I could run the institution well.

The combination still made my grade much lower than many men applying. I received no notice of the interviews. I wrote the director to ask why. He sent a letter (which I still have) stating they only sent notices to the top ten candidates. This was within their rights. I knew what that meant. They had someone in mind. These positions were high enough to become political. The Boss wrote a letter to the administrators recommending me. Other than the Boss, I knew RCC better than anyone else. It would have been a very smooth transition. This fact apparently did not make a difference. I heard rumors that a young man from Algoa Correctional Center (a men's prison on the outskirts of Jefferson City) was being considered. His wife worked for the governor at that time. Makes you wonder, but in government, it's never surprising.

Very quickly the younger man with less experience was announced as superintendent II and head of RCC. He went on the payroll June 1, 1990, but immediately took a two-week vacation. I received a letter I would be acting superintendent until he started. I was, of course, disappointed but not surprised. A great promotional opportunity was now gone. I had worked at RCC as second in command for sixteen years. Was the "good ole boy" system still alive and well? Readers may draw their own conclusion.

I'm self-motivated. I work for my own satisfaction, not someone else's. I am somewhat of a perfectionist. I also know when it is not in my best interest to exhaust myself. I did pitch right in to ensure a smooth running institution. I ran that institution as if it were mine. At least 95 percent of the staff was behind me. They supported me as they had supported the Boss.

During those weeks, there was a threat of evacuation because the river was rising. This took close monitoring. We survived and did not have to move. One night I was called by the control center officer stating there was a fire in the laundry. I asked if the fire department had been called. The officer said, "Oh, I forgot." They were called immediately. I was on my way out to RCC. The laundry was almost destroyed but was later rebuilt.

The worst-case scenario would be an escape or a death while I was in charge. The escape did not happen, but the death did. A long-term female inmate with a history of asthma died as the night nurse was trying to help her. I came running out to RCC again. What an uproar. All of Central Office had to be called, along with the coroner. To make sure I was doing everything by policy, I reviewed the books. They were all over the desk when the assistant director came in to check on our operations. I was upset because policy did not dictate some of the steps.

The assistant director said, "Don't worry, Jo Ann. You will be fine" and I was. I handled the institution well. During those two weeks, I handled many emergencies. The inmates were hard to settle down.

Have you ever been to a pauper's funeral? If not, avoid that experience. The dead woman had no family who would claim her. I am sure they were afraid of the expenses of her death. They came forward after the burial with a lawsuit, which was dismissed. The state paid for a box of cardboard (as standard) called a casket. She was buried in the place for indigent people. The staff took up a collection, inmates contributed money too, and RCC bought an arrangement of flowers. When I entered the funeral home, I was shocked. Nothing was in the room but her cardboard box on a stand and our flowers. Several of us attended the graveside ceremony. We watched that box go into the ground. It was a rainy day, and the water gushed into the hole. What would happen to a cardboard box placed in all of that water? We did the best we could. Another incident I had to put out of my mind.

After my survival of a threat of flood, a fire, and a death, the new guy arrived. My mother had already given him the nickname "the Pup." That was my mother's somewhat sarcastic sense of humor. She was as disappointed as I was. I knew the new guy had heard rumors about my wanting the position, so I met with him privately, and I told him I did want the position. I saw no reason to lie. I assured him my feelings would not in any way affect how I would work for him. Other staff told him the same thing. He had never worked with female offenders. He seemed willing to learn and work with us. He did seem to rely on my knowledge.

Soon after the superintendent II came, a custody member and his little clique started putting ideas in the Pup's mind against me. This custody member disliked me because I was briefly involved with his wife's (this was before they were married) termination from RCC. His wife had had some type of romantic involvement with a female inmate. There was good evidence to terminate her. I also had to call him down in a staff meeting because he jumped up and started ranting about something. He was one of the men who did not like female authority figures. His clique supported him and the games began. This started a period in my career when I thought I would eventually have a nervous breakdown.

Before I discuss the negative things which happened to me, I will give information on some interesting happenings. An author named Donna Ferrato was interested in battered women at that time. She wrote the book *Living with the Enemy*. She completed a later version with some of our female inmates, which came out in 2000. She was allowed to move freely in the institution to learn more about female inmates who were battered, and she was permitted to spend the night at RCC. The book was published (I have a copy). The last chapter was devoted to RCC inmates. I knew each of them. Were they all battered? That is the claim. I know it happens, but reading the files of some inmates makes one believe they are not all innocent. We will never know for sure.

Because RCC was continuing to develop, I chaired many committees. I was chairperson of the RCC hiring committee. My experience and good record-keeping became very valuable. I testified for the department and the attorney general's office on many suits concerning hiring. Every lawsuit I testified for was successful. An assistant attorney general worked with me many times. She wanted me on the stand because I was "compelling and credible." She gave me the best recommendation I ever had and I cherish it today.

ATTORNEY GENERAL OF MISSOURI

JEFFERSON CITY

JEREMIAH W. (JAY) NIXON
ATTORNEY GENERAL

65102

P.O. Box 899
(573) 751-3321

April 7, 1999

RE: Reference for JoAnn Mertens

To Whom It May Concern:

I am writing this letter of reference on behalf of JoAnn Mertens. I routinely represent the Missouri Department of Corrections in my capacity as senior litigation counsel in the Litigation Division for the Office of the Attorney General. It is in that capacity that I came to know and work with Ms. Mertens. She assisted me in the successful defense of several employment discrimination claims against the Department. As an Assistant Superintendent, Ms. Mertens had participated in a number of the hiring decisions that were at issue.

Ms. Mertens' testimony proved instrumental in persuading the jury that the hiring processes were fair and equal for all candidates considered. She was very articulate and credible. Her testimony was compelling and persuasive because she has risen from a clerk through the custody ranks to the position of Assistant Superintendent. In the course of her career she has strived to improve herself through diligence, hard work, education and training and has demonstrated a willingness to confront new challenges. The jury members perceived her to be honest, fair, reasonable, organized, and attentive to detail. In addition, she maintained excellent records which documented the interview committees' comments and considerations concerning each of the candidates evaluated.

Ms. Mertens' successful rise within the Department, her training and education, and her years of experience make her ably qualified for any number of positions. She will prove an asset in whatever career she chooses to pursue upon leaving the Missouri Department of Corrections.

Sincerely,

ral

I also testified when the corrections officers union sued the DOC. It was difficult because our attorney at that time did not know the right questions to ask to help me give an accurate account. I finally asked the committee I was testifying before if I could explain the situation in my own words. I did. We won. Others did testify too—I don't want to make the reader think I was the only one in DOC who was a good witness. This is only a personal account.

One unusual situation regarding staff came to mind when a male supervisor walked up to one of his female subordinates and kissed her on the lips in front of inmates. The female staff member sued the supervisor for harassment. I was called as a witness for the male supervisor. He was my peer. I was waiting to testify at the hearing when the male supervisor walked up to me. I plainly told him that he did not want me to testify because my testimony would do him no good. I was excused before I ever made it to the stand. I don't even remember the outcome, but I believe he got off lightly. I cannot imagine how he thought my testimony would help him.

On the other end of the witness issue, I was sued, along with many staff, by male inmates. I cannot remember any suit involving me filed by the female inmates. The suit could be as simple as not allowing a suggestive magazine in, or alleged cruelty to an inmate. Assistant superintendents place their signature on many documents. I had pending cases against me when I retired but luckily, I did not have to come back to testify. I had my share of sitting on the witness stand during my career.

Now I will go back to the fun things. I was the chairperson of the personnel committee. This group voted for an outstanding employee of the month. It was usually very satisfying for me to chair this important committee, but I will later give a very bad experience for me in this area. The committee I enjoyed most was the cultural diversity committee. This committee, consisting of staff and inmates, planned cultural events each month. We managed to find something to celebrate. We celebrated Black History Month with several events. I attended Kwanzaa for the first time. I also attended a Jewish Seder. I was invited to a Wiccan ceremony, but I felt I could not attend due to my religious beliefs. I witnessed the dedication of a sweat lodge. Women's History Month was fun. We had many speakers and other activities. Inmate groups/meetings I supervised and attended were all a pleasure to be a part of. The Longtimers group was for male inmates who were at the end of long sentences. They felt they had much different experiences than the "revolving-door" inmates. I received a personalized cigarette lighter from the Long Timers. I was a part of the NAACP group at my institution. I received a plaque from them, the Longtimers, and Parents and Their Children. I attended Ramadan and helped plan the month of celebration for the Nation of Islam.

I was a member of the department policy and procedure development committee. This committee wrote policies for the whole department. I felt belonging was a privilege. I also wrote policy and procedure for two of the institutions I was assigned to. When a central hiring committee was developed for corrections officers, I was a member of that committee also. I seemed to be appointed to many committees and employee performance reviews. I didn't mind. Most knew I kept excellent records. I also was fair, firm, and consistent. The duties helped me to broaden my knowledge of corrections.

After my promotion to superintendent I, I had to attend more executive staff meetings in the absence of the superintendent II. This monthly meeting consisted of the director, assistant directors, and institution heads. I liked going to these meetings. During the latter part of my career, a few women had been appointed institution heads or assistants. I noticed they were very quiet at these meetings. No questions or comments.

I clearly recall at one meeting, the director went around the room to ask for comments. When he came to me, he said, "Jo Ann, I know you have something to say." And I did. I was not shy anymore. At another meeting, there was a heated discussion about health services transportation. A committee had gone to much trouble to create a policy for transporting inmates to various health services. I again spoke up. I told everyone in the meeting that the plan would not work. The planners had forgotten the female inmates. They tried to think of how to incorporate them. The discussion became more heated, with me standing my ground on the issues. The director finally was tired of listening, so he said that we would table this policy and discuss it at a later time. The policy was never implemented.

Back when the Boss was institutional head, there were rumors of a male officer (who was also a preacher) having sex with female inmates in the hallway between two housing units at RCC. The Boss was furious. He did everything in his power to bring the truth of these rumors to light. Finally in July 1990, (after the Boss had retired) the officer resigned in bad standing. In August 1990, an inmate I will call Mert was released from RCC. She had been our cleaner, and we had become fond of her. She had met a man at RCC when it was co-correctional whom she later married. Mert called me in September 1990, saying she wanted to see how RCC was doing. I had heard a rumor she was pregnant when she left RCC. I asked her if she was pregnant and she said she was a little over two months. I quickly did my math and knew it could not be her husband's baby. I asked who the baby belonged to. She said an officer. I kept talking with her. She finally said, "You know who the baby belongs to." I mentioned the name of the resigned officer, and she confirmed my suspicions. She confirmed that it was under the same circumstances as we had heard.

She said her husband knew about the baby. They had decided to give it up for adoption. She appeared very upset when she talked to me. I knew she wanted this off her chest. She said she had wanted to come to me before she left RCC but was afraid she would not be released. I felt very badly that she did not trust me enough to tell me at RCC. This sexual contact between officer and inmate had done this woman a great disservice. I did not hear from Mert again.

Another one of our cleaners (female) seemed very upset while she was working for us. She finally told us an old volunteer preacher had fondled her. I believed her story. An investigation was conducted. It was found the preacher did indeed fondle her but had a "spiritual excuse" for this. He was terminated. I wonder how many other women this happened to who did not come forward. Volunteer clergy will be discussed later in the book.

Contact, mental or physical, is a way of life when males and females are in such close proximity. It is never right, but it happens. Sometimes investigations cannot produce truth. There were many times inmates tried to have staff fired and sometimes succeeded. My truth was never to be alone with any inmate. If I brought an inmate into my office, I either left the door open with me in full view or I asked someone to sit in with me. I will move back in time for a moment to the group Reaching Out. We were having a group session with teenagers. During this time, one inmate looked at me and winked. This was not good. It gave him control over me. It must be dealt with. I did not say anything until after the group was over. I brought him in my office, along with the woman who helped me. I must admit I raked him over the coals. He apologized. I could have sent him to the hole, but I chose not to. I think the lesson was better learned by the way I handled it. There were no more problems with him or any other member of the group. Word spreads in a prison setting. This female superintendent would tolerate no innuendos.

In the late eighties and early nineties, my son had worked his way through a bachelor of science degree in physics and a master's degree at University of Missouri-Rolla. He is very intelligent. His place of employment paid for the BS degree while he worked full time. He received the degree in record time. He went on a fellowship to UMR for his masters also in physics. He had settled down from his teenage years. He married and moved to Rolla. The trip took over an hour but the our family visited weekly. I missed them terribly, but my work and my mother kept me busy. Work conditions for me were terrible after the Boss retired.

My mother was diagnosed with lung cancer in 1992. She was given five months to live. She hung on with a reasonable quality of life for three years. My son had accepted a full fellowship at Georgia Institute of Technology in Atlanta. His family moved again. He was now working toward a PhD in physics. I felt very alone with no backup; however, I always wanted my son to be the best he could be. He was self-motivated like I was. I thought he would follow my footsteps in corrections but he marched to the tune of his own drummer. He appeared to be nearly a genius in math and physics. The family will be discussed more later in the book.

I had problems until I transferred to Central Missouri Correctional Center (CMCC) in 1997. I don't want to put a negative slant to this book. I am simply reporting what happened to me as I see it during my career. Everything I say in this book, other than stories about inmates, has paper backup. I have a large folder of DOC paperwork I will never throw away.

As I said earlier, a clique began to form around the Pup. The man who should have sought my advice mistrusted me. He knew that I knew the institution better than he did. He also knew I had many loyal employees behind me. I continued to work very hard. I would complete any job he assigned me to the best of my ability. One terrible mistake he made was when he allowed a member of the media (the author mentioned earlier- Donna Feratto) to stay in a female housing unit overnight. I cautioned about the liability, but he allowed it anyway. Later, when I was acting superintendent, the same media person asked to spend the night. I sought the approval of one of the assistant directors. He sent me a memo saying, "Absolutely not. There's too much liability for DOC." I already knew that. I have that memo. I sent a copy to my boss, probably out of bitterness. He ignored it.

Another incident I recall was signing of performance appraisals. Each person was evaluated yearly. (I might add that my performance appraisal dropped from highly successful to successful after the Boss left.) I was responsible for completing all performance appraisals of staff under my supervision. The superintendent II would then give his approval or make changes. The Major (chief of custody) was one of the best I had known. He always received a highly successful rating. I was told by the Pup, that he would not sign a highly successful rating for the Major. This reasoning had to do with the influence of the clique but, in addition, the Major was involved in a promotional interview process several years before at another institution. The Pup was not given the position he wanted at that time. He apparently held a grudge against the Major.

I completed the Major's appraisal as usual with highly successful. I also attached a note saying I could find no reason to drop the score. The Pup would have to override it. He did not change the score. The appraisal was processed as usual. Guess what—I made a copy of the performance appraisal with my note on it. I have it today. A copy went to the Major after he retired. I had my own code of ethics and I wouldn't break it.

There were so many instances of harassment, intimidation, and just regular wrong-doing that related directly back to the clique. For example, upper management of RCC was allowed to take a state car home with them. I took an old station wagon home daily. In one instance, one of the clique claimed I hit his personal vehicle with the state car. Interestingly, another member of the clique claimed to have witnessed it. How convenient. After I was through with my reports and conversations, nothing further was done. I saw many staff railroaded and sometimes fired who did not deserve it. I also saw staff who were friends with the clique get by with almost anything. Every lunch hour was a gathering for the clique at the gymnasium. I did not participate.

An officer was accused of familiarity with the female inmates. The investigation proved nothing. The officer transferred to another institution shortly after the investigation, and he was later fired for the same thing. The investigator, incidentally, was a large part of the clique, and loyalty to the clique prevailed. My own secretary would not work for me. She changed personnel records and allowed the investigator to access locked personnel files. This was under my supervision, but I could do nothing about it because I had no backing. She appeared to have quite a crush on the Pup.

One well-known man came in to visit a female inmate with a long sentence. I suspected something wrong and wrote a memo about it, which was ignored. Later the man was arrested for molesting a child. This inmate's child had been with him many times. Sometimes I became very tired of not being listened to. Documentation was the key and I did that. If any bad publicity came, I would know my back side was covered.

Another time, a country band came in with family ties to a female inmate with the fifty-year stip. This happened twice. Both times, I objected for security reasons. I made sure the Major set up special security measures to prevent escapes. I covered my fanny. This inmate eventually caused me to receive the only reprimand of my career. She was very manipulative and knew how to play people. Women can read other women like a book. I had this inmate and several others pegged as problems.

If you remember, I chaired the employee of the month committee. The Pup wanted my secretary/personnel clerk to be nominated, and he subtly told me so. When the committee came together, we found there was a black officer who had nearly sacrificed his life during the last flood. Everyone on the committee wanted this officer to be nominated, and I submitted the recommendation with good justification for the choice. This superintendent actually put in a written memo that I circumvented his wishes, but he felt he couldn't change it because the nominee was a black man. I sent a memo back offering to resign from the committee. He said he would not permit me to do so. When would he learn I am my own person? He did not give in. We had dual employees that month—the personnel clerk and the black officer. I am glad I owed no one anything. Being friends and also being a supervisor is difficult. I dealt with it, but he could not.

We had lots of fun times at RCC because staff was that way. We worked hard and partied harder when possible. My fiftieth birthday was a big bash. I had a large runner with most staffs' names on it. I had a great cake. Lots of people attended and to top it off, several of the male staff dressed in hula skirts and danced for me. That was a hoot. One guy sat on my lap but did not give me a lap dance. It made the Big 50 better for me. I remember I was also at work for the Big 40 and asked the Boss to let me go home. He told me staff had surprises for me, but I went home anyway. Forty was my hardest birthday.

I finally met with the Pup and his supervisor, an assistant director because I thought I could not tolerate anymore. I got a lot off my chest but nothing changed. During this time, my mother was having chemotherapy for her cancer. My son and his family were far away. I was beginning menopause and it was not kind to me. The stress was so bad I developed nightly insomnia. No medication helped. I still trudged to work and pushed myself to the maximum.

The emergency squad (referred to as e-squad) was a carefully selected group of custody staff with a leader. This squad was trained and armed when necessary. They were called on for many types of situations, such as the desegregation of MSP many years ago. As assistant superintendent, I was the administrative commander of the e-squad. It was mostly a title and only minimal supervision was required of me. The squad had to qualify each year with a physical agility test including push-ups, leg lifts, bench press, the famous twelve-minute-mile run, and other activities.

One day at a meeting, one of the members challenged me to try to pass the physical qualifications. I do not run from a challenge. I told the squad to give me one year. I would do it. A very physically fit member scoffed and said I could not do it. I was already lifting weights after I quit smoking and walking miles a day. I simply stepped it up a lot and prepared. They did not forget. In one year, I took the test. I lifted more weight than most of the women on the squad and could leg press three-hundred eighty pounds. I did the push-ups and other requirements.

The twelve-minute mile was the biggest challenge. I was not a runner. One female member tried to stay with me all the way. I told her to go on so she would not fail. I ran, I jogged, and walked fast. I was at the end of my endurance at fifty-three years old. A captain was monitoring the time of the mile. He kept pushing me to go on. Finally a squad member said to stop me because I had made it. I passed. I also gained the respect of the whole squad. My superintendent II commended me. A form letter was sent out as verification of passing. I got the letter signed by the director of adult institutions. I doubt he even noticed that a superintendent I had passed the test. I felt very good and was proud of myself.

The department decided quite a number of upper-level staff had to qualify each year with firearms. I do not like firearms. Until the first test, I had never held a gun in my hand. We had to qualify on the handgun, rifle, and the shotgun. The first time I tried the handgun, I had to shoot 150 rounds in order to qualify. I finally figured out I was not sighting it properly, but even then it was still difficult for me. The shotgun—no problem. I was a tall, largely built woman. I was almost the only woman who could remain standing and walk away without bruises when finished. We had to qualify with the rifle standing up, on one knee, and lying on the ground. I had little trouble hitting the target, but because I'm left-handed, the hot casing hit me on the arm every time. It burned me when I was lying on the ground. I continued to improve each year but refused to take a firearm home. I kept my qualifying card with me. I had met another challenge and it felt good.

The years 1993 through 1995 were almost the breaking point for me. My strength was waning. Something new, and

I thought exciting, came on the horizon. The first female director of the Missouri Department of Corrections was appointed by the governor. I knew this was the time for women in DOC—for women and blacks, but not for me personally. Still I continued to push the system. What else could happen in this career of mine? Oh, there were several things. The new director was on a mission to build new prisons. The economy was good. I had hope for my career. During the nineties, they started building a new female prison in Vandalia, which was at least two hours away from my home in a small town. What would I do when the time came? I did not want to move my ill mother from her family. I need not have worried. The situation changed so greatly that the circumstances provided an answer. The reader will see this soon.

The Pup was a stickler for written policy. He was not satisfied with our present flood policy and procedure. The staff toiled over it to make it acceptable to him, although we tried to tell him we could not develop a policy with every possible scenario for floods—each flood is unique. We had to plan as the flood progressed. We assured him that all staff knew what to do and could accomplish the task no matter what. He still persisted. We worked until we developed a procedure that seemed to satisfy him with what he thought covered *everything* about a flood at RCC. No one had ever experienced "the five-hundred-year flood."

June and October are typically flood months in Missouri. In June 1993 that Missouri River became a force to be reckoned with. The river may not look big but it is deep, swift, muddy, and spreads across the river bottom. RCC was situated in the river bottom. The rain kept pouring down and the water kept rising. It had to be monitored around the clock. This was the first flood experience for the Pup. He looked at his well-thought-out flood procedure. He assumed everything would be all right. (RCC is located near the water tower in the picture shown below.)

The preparations began. Buses were secured. Inmates and staff were put on alert. Overcrowding—and the fact that the new female facility was not completed—put a kink in the plans. No one knew where to place these female inmates. Record-breaking flood levels were predicted for the river. It was being called the "five-hundred-year flood" which means a flood of this magnitude only occurred once every five hundred years. RCC had never experienced this. Everyone involved was getting nervous. The staff was confident—we had done it many times, thus we could do it again.

There was an institution across the river that was formerly known as Church Farm, because it was also a farm in its early years. It was then called Central Missouri Correctional Center. CMCC was a thousand-bed facility for minimum and medium security men. Outside of the main perimeter fence was a small minimum security unit (MSU). It was like a mini-institution. MSU was a part of CMCC and housed four hundred of the inmates. It was determined that MSU was the best place for the bulk of the women. The minimum security men had to be transferred first to other institutions. You can only imagine the task to transfer four hundred men and four hundred women at the same time. The high-security females were placed on lock down (total confinement) in the Fulton Diagnostic Center for Men (FRDC). RCC officers had to cover this new post. Women nearing release would be sent to community release centers in St. Louis and Kansas City, but these centers first had to be set up to accommodate women.

The whole department was in an uproar, including the female offenders. Some offenders knew what was happening, but others did not. The women were always a bit more excited and anxious than male inmates about a move such as this. No one at this time had any idea what type of flood to expect. Each woman was told to bring what she could fit in a pillowcase. I don't have to mention that caused quite an outcry—women have "things."

The staff at CMCC was working overtime also, to remove the men. CMCC staff had to clean the place before the women arrived. RCC staff would take over the security and staffing of the CMCC minimum-security unit. The superintendent III at CMCC (I will refer to him as Boss II) would have nothing to do with the supervision; however, coordination and cooperation was necessary. RCC received that cooperation from CMCC. In a crisis, employees always worked together for the common good.

The move proceeded with buses lining up. Files and all administrative offices had to be moved to an upper level of the building; food had to be moved out of the institution. All work areas were evacuated and secured. The job was tremendous, but for RCC we all pulled together. We had done it before, and we knew we could do it again. We did not think past the move out. At the time of the move, several institutions sent their armed emergency squads to help our squad. The squads are necessary to control inmates in crisis situations. They did make the women nervous.

I walked the grounds trying to calm the women. One incident upset me greatly. A woman was not in the direct line-up so one of the squad members pointed a gun at her and ordered her to get back in line. I told the officer this wasn't necessary and he retreated. This officer was big, fully dressed in uniform, pointing a gun and, I felt, being a macho man when the circumstances didn't warrant it. That unnecessary action could have started a volatile situation. This was not unusual for some of the male officers, but not on my watch.

In June and July, it's very hot and muggy in Missouri. Staff was working almost around the clock. I was exhausted—my mother was sick, my dog was old, and I still had insomnia and the effects of menopause. I was not sure I could endure but my mom was good at pep talks and very understanding.

After we had all of the female inmates settled in, we had to establish another institution as we had so many times before. New policy and procedure had to be implemented, because everything had changed. After the shock wore off, I began to settle in, but the new institution was not RCC. I went into the office of the Pup. He was pale, nervous, and completely exhausted. He appeared to not know what to do next. One of his family members had been ill and he, too, had personal concerns. I knew we, the administration, had to pull together. I asked the superintendent II to come with me in the state car to ride to the Fulton Reception & Diagnostic Center to check on the inmates we had housed there. I wanted him to get away which allowed me to talk with him. With all of the problems I had with his clique, I still did not want RCC to fail. It was my baby. On the way over, I gave him a stern pep talk. I told him the staff at RCC was remarkable. I asked him to let them do their jobs. We would survive this. I think he took my talk to heart and seemed better when we returned.

The flood waters continued to rise. The water completely destroyed our business office which was in a house, not in the RCC compound. The water was seeping up to the second floor of the administration/housing unit building where the files, all paperwork, and some inmate property was located. We had never had to move items above second floor before. This was unheard of. I had ridden back into RCC on a backhoe several times with water circling around me. A backhoe was now insufficient. Debris was floating everywhere. Disease was a real threat. A cadre made of mostly men and a few women went in by boat to move certain items to the third floor, bring out the pertinent paperwork, and salvage as much inmate property as possible. This operation took days to accomplish. It was a very nasty job. I did not go back in, because with my mother on chemotherapy, I felt I could not take germs to her. I was criticized for this, but I held fast. I felt I had done enough for the cause. My job was to stay at the new institution to make it work for us. The water level took weeks to go down making the surrounding property free of water. The damage was tremendous for the entire river bottom. A small town was lost forever.

CHIEF OF CUSTODY after flood

Much later, after all the water had gone down, I went to RCC to see for myself. It was a disaster. I think I cried. I walked to the steps which led down to the administrative offices, which were always in the basement. The paneling was ruined. I developed severe mold allergies which I attribute to the nasty flood waters through the years. Ironically, there in the mud lay the RCC flood plan. It was the plan the Pup had worked so hard on. No one could possibly have planned for a flood of this magnitude. In later years, I came back to Jefferson City for a RCC reunion. Many staff participated. As a part of our memories, we toured the old building. It had then been bought by a farmer in the area. This is how close the staff was and how they cared for this institution and other employees. Now many are retired, dead, or somewhere unknown. Some are still working at central office or institutions around the state.

The small institution at CMCC had some advantages. It had more work for the inmates. Prison Industries had several training/work programs there including Quick Print and Tire Recycling. These jobs paid more than the menial work inside the fence. Security had to be beefed up, but soon we were back to running an institution. We didn't know at that time that RCC was almost completely destroyed. We were not going back; but we had always gone back.

The reality was *we were not going back to the institution we loved.* The director of DOC decided that RCC would not be rebuilt again. The new women's institution was in the making. The Boss, even though retired, offered to supervise the rebuilding of RCC. No way. Bigger and better institutions had to be built in rural areas to provide jobs. This restructuring relocated many inmates away from their homes and families in the St. Louis, Kansas City, and Springfield areas.

Now what would I do? I did not want to leave the Jefferson City area because of my mom, her family, friends; it was also the only home I'd ever known. Our director did a remarkable thing. She gave all RCC employees a priority transfer, which meant staff could move into the same job classification at any institution they chose. They had priority over all candidates, even if those candidates were in line for a promotion. This was a God-send to all of us. With my superintendent I position, I would have fewer choices than the others because fewer positions were being vacated. Apparently I was not going to be promoted. I bided my time and waited.

In 1993, a new position, constituent services coordinator, became available at our central office. I read the qualifications. I met each and every one of them. It did not even require a college degree. I applied, thinking maybe I should get out of the institution business and try a central office position. An interview was scheduled. My mother encouraged me. She even bought me a new black suit so I would look professional and sharp. I thought I did. The day of the interview I was sick, dizzy, and almost anemic from the effects of menopause. I kept the appointment anyway. The interview went well, I thought. The director was gracious. It looked promising. Soon after, it was announced that a secretary to one of the assistant directors was given the position. She was young, no college experience, and just a bit of experience in dealing with families of the inmates. Again, politics raised its ugly head. I will say she appears to be doing well today. No hard feelings about the person who got it, but bitterness was taking over. I made an appointment with the director. She heard me out. I asked if a promotion was anywhere in the future for me. I clearly remember her turning her head away from me. She said she believed in education and the college degree. I told her I certainly did also, because I had a son who was nearing completion of a PhD in physics, and I added that experience could not be replaced in the correctional field. What you learn in a textbook is not like living it. I left feeling the meeting was for naught.

I trudged on. During the time the women inmates were located behind CMCC, it was determined they were using too much toilet paper. This was true. They would stuff dolls and animals with the toilet paper. They also had many other uses for it. The Pup decided to ration toilet paper to one personal roll per week. Additional rolls would still be issued as necessary.

Sometime after the new restriction on toilet paper, a complaint from one of the inmates leaked out through the use of pay phones in the housing units. They could only place collect calls. A female inmate called the National Organization for Women (NOW). I had to speak with them on the phone to explain our reasoning for the change. They did not like my answer; one spokesperson said my salary should be taken to supply toilet paper to the inmates. NOW sent a month's supply of toilet paper to the institution to prove their point. A local newspaper printed an article shown below. Dealing with radical groups and the media was my least favorite duty. Dealing with the legislature could also be burdensome; however, some were very gracious and understanding. They had to respond to their constituents. I became friends with one of the first female legislators at that time and she was very helpful to our plights.

• TUESDAY, AUGUST 20, 1991

On A Roll

Renz Prison Rations Toilet Paper; NOW Comes To Women's Rescue

By Terry Ganey
Post-Dispatch Jefferson City Bureau Chief

JEFFERSON CITY — The National Organization for Women has delivered 360 rolls of toilet paper to the Renz Correctional Center, a women's prison where inmates have been put on a ration of one roll a week.

NOW state coordinator Mary Mosley said female prisoners were being shortchanged. She said NOW's gift "won't last for a long time, but it will at least show our good faith with the women there."

Mosley, who lives in Fulton, said the organization was concerned about the problems of women in prison. She said the shipment of toilet paper was delivered Saturday to the prison, which houses about 320 female inmates.

The Post-Dispatch mentioned the rationing in a column last week on state budget cuts. Mosley said she believed women used an average of more than one roll a week.

Mosley said the issue had struck a responsive chord among the organization's members because they had talked about "restroom equity" at a recent workshop. The issue concerns the number of women's restroom facilities in public places, compared to the number for men.

A bill that would have increased the number of women's toilet facilities in public places failed in the last legislative session.

Jo Ann Mertens, assistant superintendent at Renz, said the prison appreciated the gift, which amounts to a week's supply. But she said the state had provided an adequate supply.

"If necessary, they do have access to toilet paper," Mertens said. "In addition to the personal roll that they are given once per week, there is also toilet paper at their work sites."

Mertens said the paper rationing began a year ago as a way to save money. She said inmates had been using toilet paper for such things as stuffing homemade dolls and cleaning windows.

"I would like to say I am sympathetic toward women's needs, but I also know there is a lot of abuse of materials," Mertens said, adding: "I'm sure if someone was totally out of toilet paper, more would be issued."

In 1994, I interviewed for a superintendent II position at CMCC. I did not get the position. It was filled by a black man who had less experience than I had. I was tired of this. I filed a discrimination suit with the EEOC (Equal Employment Opportunity Commission). I sited discrimination based on both gender and race. I had what I felt was quite a bit of proof. After months of waiting, I received my answer. No validity to the suit. The upper management hiring committee (who held the interviews) *failed* to keep records. This was the EEOC's reason to deny the suit. As a person who was responsible for many hirings during my employment, I kept concise records of everyone whom our committee interviewed (as the chairperson). I do have a letter of recommendation from the attorney's office stating I helped the Department of Corrections win many lawsuits due to my record keeping.

If I had not kept records, I would have been terminated. How, then, can the upper management of a division be allowed to not keep adequate records of hiring? I have copies of my suit and the reason for dismissing it. Still, just making the attempt gave me some satisfaction. The person who was hired in this position was later let go because of his harassment of female officers. Who would have been the better candidate and how was this person selected?

My home situation was becoming much worse in 1995. My mother had decided to stop her chemotherapy. The cancer returned quickly. My son was supposed to receive his PhD in physics from Georgia Institute of Technology in Atlanta in September 1995. For some unknown reason, my son's advisor said he would not receive the PhD until December 1995. I panicked. My mother was hanging on to life so she could see him receive this honor. I wanted to call the advisor, but my son did not want me to do it. I respected his wishes; however, my mother did not live to see him receive his PhD.

In September 1995, an opening for superintendent I came at the institution we were connected to (CMCC). I jumped at the chance to get out while I could. I submitted my prioritized transfer. It was a hard decision for me to make because RCC was my work home for twenty years. I knew I did not want to transfer to Vandalia when the new female institution was built. The completion was near.

The Pup received a big promotion during that time. He left almost immediately. Our little unit (RCC) was placed under the superintendent III of CMCC. I will refer to him as Boss II. I would continue to run this unit until a superintendent was picked for the new female institution and trained at RCC. Again, my plans were put aside for the good of the division. My transfer was held for me. This superintendent III (Boss II) had worked at RCC when I was a corrections officer II and he a parole officer. I had also worked with his father at MSP. Both were great guys with integrity.

RCC ran very well under my direction and that of the CMCC superintendent. One event did cause me to receive the only reprimand of my career. It was devastating to me. In November 1995, I was advised by the nursing supervisor that we had a serious louse problem. This is not uncommon in an institution. I had dealt with this issue when the males were at RCC. This time the outbreak was found in all housing units. A professional from the state health department told us the only way to eradicate the problem was to wash all personal property and disinfect all persons. It must be done immediately.

We had all been through this, so we started what would be a twenty-four-hour job. All washable personal effects were taken to the laundry. Our honor-dormitory inmates were not happy. This housing unit had many of the fifty-year stips in it. One of the inmates I mentioned before had connections to the clergy and volunteers on the outside. We met with the inmates on this housing unit. It was agreed they would cooperate. We promised we would do the best we could. Dressing inmates in paper gowns was standard procedure; however, no official policy covered this. Some of the larger inmates preferred large trash bags and were given them. Finally the remaining inmates were placed in trash bags when all institutions ran out of paper gowns. There was no way of finding paper gowns late at night.

That evening things appeared to be going well. Our staff had the situation under control. My aging dog was at home alone because my mother took care of him when I was working. My mother had died on October 9, 1995. I called every neighbor and friend to ask them to check on my dog. I found no one at home. I knew he needed to be fed, was in the dark, and needed to go outside. I called Boss II with a report of how well the situation was going. He gave me permission to go home. I went home to my poor dog. I was so exhausted I did not go back. I did check with the institution several times through the night and all was well. The job was completed by early morning.

One of the women who was serving fifty years without parole got word to the local newspaper. The department executives were put on the spot and reacted, in my opinion, without giving a thought to the dedicated staff. I watched the news on TV. The governor at that time and the department director stated whoever was responsible for this carelessness might lose their jobs. I was so surprised and stressed when I heard those statements. To hear those statements on TV with no warning crushed me. Our reports were in. The job was done well. You have to understand with politics, one must CYOB. That did not make me feel any better.

Boss II told me not to worry about it. He assured me the job was well done. It was still a humiliation to me because this incident was leaked to the media. By January 1996 I thought the incident had been forgotten until Boss II told me to expect a letter of reprimand. He was also getting one. He and I were both furious. The long letter of reprimand came from the Department of Adult Institutions director. It was hurtful. It was the only reprimand of my career. I wrote a letter back with an explanation and an apology. I have these letters today. I apologized only for my decision to leave the institution that night. I told the director I left that night "to handle what an employer would see as an insignificant personal problem at home." The problem, of course, was the care of my aging dog. I have never made public my true reason for leaving until I wrote this book. My dog died five months after my mother, at my side in the middle of the night. I believe it was from a broken heart because of being alone so much.

Boss II believed in my ability to run the female unit, so I did just that. It was a strain on me with my mother's sickness, but I felt it was my responsibility to be at work every day. I arranged for a woman to come in to be with my mother when I was at work. If I had it to do over, I would have taken the large amount of leave I had accumulated to be with my mother.

October 5, 1995, was my mother's eighty-eighth birthday. She was doing poorly that day. I told her I would stay with her, but she knew my responsibilities. She told me she would be all right. She had told me earlier if she ever went into the hospital again she would not come out. My mother was a very strong and wise woman. Later that day, I received a call she had been taken to the hospital. I visited her that evening. It was obvious she was failing. The next day at work, I felt I needed to call the Boss to tell him about my mother. Since his retirement, he helped seniors in the community. My mom was a friend of his. There was no answer at his home. I thought that was very unusual, but I was busy and let it go.

Later that day, my good friend, the Major, came into my office looking pale. He told me the Boss had died that day (he was being taken to the hospital as I was calling). I almost passed out but could not be looked upon as weak. I tried to go about business as usual. All staff who knew him was almost to the point of being unable to carry out their duties. I took the staff chaplain with me as I walked around the housing units telling the female inmates of the Boss's death. Most of them still knew him. They broke down as I did telling them. It was good for me to know so many staff and inmates felt my grief. Later that evening I had to tell my mother her good friend had passed away. She shared my grief even though she was almost to the point of death herself. She was eighty-eight years old, and he was sixty-one.

Early in the morning of October 9, 1995, my mother died peacefully from pneumonia, not lung cancer. Relatives and friends were with me. Dealing with two deaths in one week took its toll. My mother had talked to my son in Georgia the night before. The last word I ever heard her say was "PhD." I am still resentful she did not see the ceremony. My son and I decided he would not come home for the funeral. He might not finish his thesis in December 1995 if he took the time off. This left me alone to work out all the details. The Boss's family and I had to work out funeral arrangements because so many people knew both families. The funerals were planned for separate times.

Our emergency squad offered to be the pall bearers and color guard for my mom. It was a wonderful thing to see at my mother's funeral along with a copy of my son's incomplete thesis wrapped in pink and dedicated to her. The Boss's funeral was attended by so many people, I couldn't get into the church. I sat in the back. Still, his family had come to my mother's visitation. This was a terrible time for me and almost too much to bear. Friends and family helped but it was still all on me.

It was hard for me to go on, but corrections was also my life. I did regret not spending more time with Mom. Soon a new superintendent came to RCC in preparation for the move to the new women's prison. He was great. He knew little about female inmates but was willing to rely on me for training. He was a bit messy, though. I remember coming into his office and finding it in disarray. It looked like he lived there. I asked him politely if he remembered the director was coming to see RCC that day. He laughed and asked if he should clean up at bit. I said, "Yes!"

Soon after, RCC held interviews for the new assistant superintendent for the recently built women's prison. I was a part of that interview. I really appreciated the new superintendent for the respect he gave me. Someone to take my place was hired. Several years ago, I was visiting in Jefferson City and of course, I visited a prison. This assistant superintendent had been promoted again. He walked up to me and gave me two hugs. He said I helped jump-start his career in corrections. This man is now dead. He died well before his time.

CENTRAL MISSOURI CORRECTIONAL CENTER

1997–2000 (Retirement)

Most of the administration for the new women's prison was in place now. It was time for me to transfer to CMCC. I was given a huge party and the staff presented me with a beautiful plaque.

My emotions were all over the place. I was leaving staff whom I considered family, inmates I had watched do their time for years, and the institution I had helped build. The inscription on the plaque says it all. "Leadership, Guidance, and Support— You have built an institution that many times had to stand alone. Because of your hard work and love for Renz, it has prevailed. You have instilled in us the same type loyalty that will last forever and makes RCC unique. Whatever the future may bring, RCC will always be an old friend with fond memories." A picture of the Boss and me is on the plaque.

I actually do not remember the date I transferred to CMCC. It was in 1997. I was happy to go there because I had been able to pick my institution, which only RCC staff, with the prioritized transfer, was allowed to do. Of course, I was taking a position which would have been a promotion for someone there, so I expected resentments. One particular man, I was told, was sure he would be the superintendent I. He was allegedly not happy I was taking his position. He later worked for me. It took a bit of time, but he began to respect me. I understand his disappointment. I had lunch with him several times after I retired. He has now passed away.

CMCC was a thousand-bed medium security prison for men. I had experiences now in every level of custody of both men and women. CMCC was near the age of RCC. The institution and grounds were getting old and outdated. A new administration building had been built a few years back. I remember walking down the sidewalk the first day. Staff was standing on the outside of the administrative building. As I walked, I felt awkward because I knew very few staff. It was then I realized I was the first woman in a position of this level (middle management) *ever* at CMCC. Was the battle beginning again?

I had a small office in a crowded area. I was to supervise the classification and records section. This entailed supervision of caseworkers, their supervisors (functional unit managers), and the records section. Boss II also decided I would develop the policy and procedure for the institution. I had experience with policy and procedures at RCC. The duties of a superintendent I in an institution the size of CMCC were very different from a small institution as RCC. It was almost like a demotion in duties. There were two superintendent II"s above me in rank and then the superintendent III. I was very happy to see Boss II. As I said, we were old colleagues. He was a down-to-earth guy. I settled in. I was a hands-on supervisor. I would travel out of the administration building to the main institution to walk through the housing units. I would also visit the individual classification workers in their offices. I was not a person to sit in an office all day. I enjoyed learning about the inner workings of the institution. Soon I began to be recognized and for the most part, respected. There were many good staff at CMCC, some from RCC who had used their prioritized transfer to come to CMCC. I saw several people I already knew.

In one of CMCC housing units I saw a male inmate. I stopped. He was older and very thin—certainly time had taken its toll—but it was my old acquaintance, Porky, from when I first came to RCC. I called out his real name. He had already figured out it was me. He and I talked. I found out he had been in and out since the seventies. He had developed diabetes and was having trouble with his feet. I knew Porky would pass the word about me at CMCC. He would have my back. He sided much more with staff than inmates and everyone knew it. Boss II respected him, as I did.

In the beginning at CMCC, staff was sometimes not so kind. It was still hard for some of them to accept a woman in this position. I also had a bit of trouble with the superintendent II's getting in my business. I actually reported directly to the superintendent III but they failed to remember that. One of them was in charge of programs and the other support services. I am not sure they even got along. During my time at CMCC, I saw several superintendent II's come and go. They continued to be promoted on.

On several occasions, all superintendents but me were out of the institution. At those times, I became the head honcho. I liked being in charge. Nothing about me was shy. I had complete confidence in my management abilities. One day when I was in charge, I got word of something "going down" in the large institution. It was not being handled by policy. I called over one of the leaders of the emergency squad. I showed him our policy and told him I wanted it done that way. He said he would not do it. I believe this was because I was a woman, but I couldn't prove it. When I asked him why he wouldn't do it, he said he didn't believe it was right. I then gave him two choices. He could do as I told him to do, or I would call a higher-level custody officer to escort him off the grounds. I guess by the tone of my voice, he knew I meant it. He reluctantly did as he was told to do.

After all of these years, I had the reputation of being outspoken (and, I might add, many times I was right). We were sent to many training courses. There was one middle management supervisory training put on by the division of personnel. I went along with many of my colleagues. We were divided into groups to find answers to specific supervisory situations. After discussions as a group, we were responsible for our own answers. It was quite a session. I remember arguing about almost every scenario. No one seemed to agree with my solutions. Finally I just put down my answer as I saw it. The instructor then asked us to add up our scores. Mine was very low. He called out for the highest score to the lowest score.

When I raised my hand with the lowest score, I bowed my head in shame. To my surprise, he said the lowest score meant the best supervisory skills. I had the best score. I looked around the room at all of those supervisors with degrees and felt really good. . No one said a word to me. I don't have those scores. I wish I had asked for them. We only received a certificate.

After my mother died in 1995, my son kept asking me to move to Williamsburg, Virginia. He is employed by NASA in Hampton as a senior scientist. We spoke every week. I missed my family. Still, I loved my work. I had every possible opinion from the people I knew. I was eligible for early retirement because I started at age eighteen with the State of Missouri. I continued to ponder this decision. I had planned for retirement by being a long-term state employee, so I would receive reasonable retirement benefits and great health insurance. My pension would have been much greater if I had received the same salary as my male counterparts. Missouri was my home of almost sixty years. This decision could not be taken lightly.

I kept on with my duties at CMCC, but my heart was not in it. The pace there was so slow and laid back. I missed the adrenaline rush, as usual. In 1997, the new female prison was opened at Vandalia, Missouri. All of the women were moved out of the small institution behind the large one at CMCC. In the past, before the women came, this area was known as minimum security unit or MSU as I will refer to it. After the cleanup was complete, minimum security males began being transferred into MSU. The division moved quickly when there was space for inmates. Boss II asked if I would be willing to run the daily operations of MSU. I jumped at the chance. It would be like my own four-hundred-bed institution. He said I also had to continue as policy and procedure coordinator and continue to supervise the classification/records staff in the administration building, but that was no problem. I used our golf cart to move back and forth between the two places.

I was again a big part of rebuilding programs and jobs for the minimum security males. I had a good staff. I felt very comfortable moving my office to MSU. Still there was a conflict sometimes between my judgment and that of the two superintendent IIs, who actually supervised some of the sections of MSU. Shortly after I relocated I was happy to see that my old friend, Porky, was transferred to MSU. He was a head cook. He always made sure staff had safe and tasty meals. He would let me know what was going on in the housing units. As I said earlier, he was an OG (old gangsta).

I also met an unusual man who was called "One Arm" because he had lost one arm as a child. He was huge and very likeable. He was in prison for "accepting the earnings of a prostitute," or otherwise known as a pimp. We strong women really gave him a hard time about his profession because it was degrading to women, but he took it well. A bond developed with him and our staff. He also would let us know what was going on. I knew he had our backs. One day I had to call him in because of complaints from the inmates he was not using deodorant. We figured out a way another inmate would help him, since he only had one arm.

When I finally retired, I came back to visit CMCC the next year. One Arm was there to greet me. I almost suffocated from the one-armed hug I got. Porky was not there. I was told he had been released and died of complications of diabetes. Before I retired, Porky told me we would see each other again. Maybe in a later life.

MSU continued on with added programs and jobs for the inmates. I was always asked by inmate organizations to come to their meetings and be a part of their groups. MSU had Longtimers, NAACP, The Inmate Committee (this committee was a link between the inmate population and the administration), and others. I enjoyed being a part of this. One responsibility I had was approving inmates to go out in town on work release. This was also mentioned earlier. Some jobs were in state buildings. I took this responsibility very seriously, because of the bad press if one of these inmates did something wrong or escaped. Many times the superintendent II's had their favorites. They insisted the inmates be given work release. If I felt there was a risk, I wanted their approval on paper. I did not want my job on the line for someone else's mistake. This stance did not always set well.

MSU had a computer class inside of the security fence in a trailer. A woman had been hired to teach the computer class in March 1998. I was concerned for her safety. The trailer she worked in was isolated. This woman did not have corrections experience. I wrote of my concerns to everyone I could. In June 1998, MSU experienced a power outage. We were concerned about security thus all inmates were ordered back to their housing units. One inmate failed to return to his housing unit. No one noticed.

The computer teacher had moved to safety in the classification trailer with other staff. The inmate in question somehow talked the teacher into returning to the trailer with him. I'm not sure why other staff where she took shelter did not react, and I have no idea why the outage did not trigger a concern in my brain either. I had been worried already about this area, but I was busy helping the institution become secure. The worst happened. The woman was raped by the inmate. This inmate had ninety days till his release. You cannot always predict inmate behavior but certainly all precautions need to be in place. They were not. MSU should have had an officer patrolling those trailers but there was always a shortage of officers.

Later it was learned the inmate in question left a library book in the computer trailer subtly outlining his feelings for this teacher. She had not looked at it. Had I read what he wrote before the rape, he would have gone straight to the hole. There were many staff errors in this situation. All staff felt very bad about it.

In August and September 1998, I again wrote memorandums about safety and security. (I have documentation for all of these memos.) My first recommendation was more officers. The second one was an intercom system. These things were out of my control, but I could express my opinion. The memos were sent to the three superintendents ranking above me. Nothing was ever done. The woman who was raped came back to work after a few weeks to the same conditions. She later left the Department of Corrections to work for another state agency. There was a trial. She had to testify and the inmate was convicted of rape. I came to know this woman. She later became a friend of mine.

Several RCC former and present staff members could not forget our beloved Boss. After the new Women's Correctional Center was opened, many staff members signed a petition to dedicate a part of that facility to Bill Turner. In December 1998, our dream came to pass. The chapel at the new women's prison was dedicated to the Boss. I played a big part in the planning of the dedication. I also was one of the speakers, and I unveiled the plaque. The plaque placed in the chapel was beautiful. For a man who had changed the history of DOC, a final tribute was in place.

In 1999, before my retirement, I was again pondering my work in corrections. I thought about the inmates I had known. It was clear to me that many inmates needed a helping hand when they were released. We tried to provide them with some education and job experience. If they stayed in prison any time at all, they could not make good decisions for themselves. In a prison, you are regimented and told what to do 24/7. The loss of connection with the outside world takes its toll. I went home every night unlike the inmates. I always joked I did "life on the installment plan." I sometimes believe I took on the prison world more than the outside world. I had gone through every government take on the prison system. I saw the "lock them up and feed them" attitude. I also saw the trend to "coddle them". I had never remembered a plan for assistance after release other than parole and half-way houses. Parole was considered more punitive.

I was always a deep thinker, so my brain thought about a reentry plan. I put down on paper a plan to have a toll-free number to be given to each inmate when released. This number would be staffed by volunteers for long hours. Inmates could call for referrals, crisis situations, housing, drug treatment, etc. This bank of knowledge would have every possible referral. Using volunteers would mean the program would have minimal costs to implement. I put this idea in a letter to the director of Adult Institutions. I never received a response.

I do not have the letter; however, I shared this idea with a member of Prison Fellowship. She was also excited about it. Now reentry is big in government from the federal level down to the county level. Missouri was a trailblazer for reentry. I have now learned there are "warm cards" out there that are similar to my idea. I should have patented my idea along with another idea— consignment shops. I had that idea but never acted on it until too late. My mother introduced me to a deep dish pizza when I was in my teens. She took a box of pizza mix and baked it in a baking pan—thus deep dish. Everyone should push their ideas to the maximum. That is exactly what I intend to do with this book.

Through 1998 and 1999, I kept pushing forward. I tried to make MSU a good place for staff and inmates. Most of the staff there backed me. I had no problem generally with the inmates. It soon became boring again to me. My son continued to ask me to move to Virginia. In late 1999, I found I needed major surgery. I had this surgery in February 2000. During the recuperation, I made the difficult decision to retire early at age fifty-eight. I saw no hope of promotion. I saw little challenge for me. I missed my family. While I was off on sick leave, I gave Boss II my retirement notice. Because of doctor's orders, I did not come back to the institution other than for a retirement party and a plaque. I had broken my bridges and could not go back without being upset. I was leaving a career I loved much too early. If I could make the decision again, I would have waited several years. Looking back, I think I would have again been transferred to another institution. CMCC closed as RCC did. I officially retired on June 1, 2000. I began in corrections in June 1966.

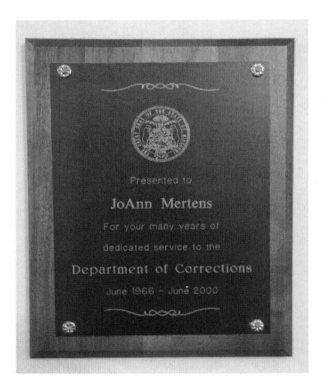

I have thought of the rise of women in Missouri Department of Corrections. There are so many more women now. I am sure their stories are much different from mine. I started in corrections at the bottom many years before them. There are four or more women in high positions in the DOC whom I know. At least three of those women started working at Renz Correctional Center many years after I started in corrections. I thought of contacting these women, but I felt they would not be willing to talk about their career ladder. Times have changed. I also thought about contacting some of the women who left without being promoted as far as their potential. A few turned me down. Many of the others are either dead or cannot be contacted. I feel alone with my experiences in Missouri Department of Corrections.

One old friend gave me permission to tell her story. In 1973, she worked at Algoa Correctional Center, west of Jefferson City. It was an all-male institution. She says she was forced out of Algoa. She was also a woman who spoke her mind. She filed for discrimination. She had to handle her own case. The same problems prevailed with her. Women made better scores on the written tests, but many institutions were not yet ready to accept a majority of female custody officers. Women were asked why they were interested in a corrections officer position. One woman was even asked by the warden to waive her place in the top ten so males could be promoted more easily. In order to keep your job, you did what you had to do. My friend was like me. We pushed for our rights.

In 1977, my friend was hired by the Boss at RCC. She quickly climbed through the custody ranks. She moved to another institution as captain in 1986. She had trouble with a high-ranking official and moved to another field. She has a bad taste in her mouth about all of these issues. She and I have remained friends.

Remembering her story made me think of another incident of mine. Using the merit system for upper-level positions, a grade was determined by a combination of experience and education, sometimes with a written test. With these factors combined to decide a score, women were lacking in experience. It was harder for them to move into the top-ten scores.

When I took my oral examination for corrections officer II (sergeant), I was asked if I would work a tower. This question was totally out of place. You usually did not work a tower in any custody position other than as a corrections officer I. I was applying for correctional officer II. The committee also wanted to know if I was planning to transfer to the female institution. I told them I intended to continue working at a male institution. One of the interview team had the nerve to ask me if I was a "women's libber." I told him I was not, but I believed in equal rights. I got the position I was hoping for.

In 2012, an article appeared in a local newspaper which said "Streep jabs Hollywood boys club." Meryl Streep blasted the film industry's statistics of 82 percent men vs. 18 percent women. These "dreadful" statistics showed "the shocking underrepresentation of women in our business." I guess corrections has come further than the movie industry, but it's still a shame there is a glass ceiling. Women show aptitudes equal to men in any profession, if given the same chance.

FROM 2000 TO PRESENT

(The Rest of The Story)

This is indeed the story of one woman at three prisons and the experiences of rising through the ranks. It is about the glass ceiling and the price women have paid when they hit that glass ceiling. My criminal justice career did not end when I retired. It is necessary that I continue the story to the end of this book. I moved to Williamsburg, Virginia, only because my family lives here. I came in early June 2000. I am not a history buff, so Colonial Williamsburg is not a favorite of mine. I like the beach but tourists and road conditions deter me from enjoying it. Williamsburg is now a city of transplants, many from the north. I feel I have nothing in common with the majority who live here. I came to Virginia knowing no one but my family. The days were long for me. The beach became tiring alone. I was in an area without a prison. I applied for several jobs. I was hired one month after I retired. I became a leasing agent for a large property management company. The job was just all right. It paid poorly, I had to work forty hours per week, and one male supervisor was allegedly addicted to pain pills. I did enjoy it when he was not there because I could work on my own. I picked up the duties easily. I stayed there for approximately one year.

Virginia is a "right to work" state which I believe involved unions and employee rights. All it means to me is that an employer can terminate a person for the wrong hair color. I found an e-mail I was not supposed to see at the leasing office. It was from a Tupperware dealer who was a friend of my female supervisor. This dealer told my supervisor she was so excited about having my job when I left, although I had said nothing about quitting. I told the property manager that I had seen the e-mail. I was then laid off because allegedly I did not want to be promoted up the ladder (funny, I was never asked). *For the first time in my life, I drew unemployment.* These circumstances made me feel ashamed. I dislike the employment laws of Virginia. The word Commonwealth was not a word I was familiar with. I was a trooper. I pushed on.

My next position was assistant shelter manager at a local domestic violence shelter. This position was twenty hours per week. It was more suitable to retirement. The work was similar to supervising a housing unit in a female institution. Yes, many of these women were battered; however, they had some of the same characteristics as inmates. I am sure some people will protest this statement, but it's my observation. I worked there for approximately one year. Once a week I worked late, and every few weeks I had to be on call. I had been on call for twenty years at DOC, so I was not excited about doing this again. The top-level manager at the shelter was an alcoholic. We all knew it but the board didn't. This woman had no mercy on staff. I had a bleed in my eye (wet macular degeneration) while working there. It was hard to drive at night after a procedure I had. At a staff meeting, shortly after I had the eye procedure, I asked if someone would take my week's duty. No one volunteered. The manager told me I would have to take it. At the same staff meeting, she told the two men who worked there that if they ever had to pick up or deal directly with a woman while on call, a female staff member would be called to perform this part of the job. A woman has to be able to do the work of a man for the same pay, right? Why were these men spared?

I went back to the shelter after the meeting and mulled this over. Again, I'd been subject to a type of reverse discrimination. I was told to continue my on-call duty even with eye problems, but the men could be relieved of their duties just because they were men. My emotions went wild. I grabbed the book we took with us when on call and the pager. I went to the main office. The manager wasn't there, but her assistant was available so I went to her. I handed her the book, the pager, and my keys. She was stunned. *Yes, I quit without notice for the first time in my life.* Someone *had* to take my call that week. The manager later was involved in a tragedy which I will not disclose. I am sorry for that.

I needed to keep busy. I started to work at a health food store. I actually liked the work, but the pay was a paltry six fifty per hour. I had found quickly this area pays nothing for the work a person is expected to do, and most jobs had no benefits. I didn't need the benefits, because I was adequately covered by the State of Missouri. I had planned for those benefits years ago. My employer at the health food store brought me some new problems. He was old, retired military, and appeared to have some dementia. One day I carried his briefcase in for him. I saw a bottle of liquor and a handgun in it. I did not ask. He could be very cranky with some of the women who worked there. He made them cry, but I didn't cry. I met him on my terms. He told me once he could fire me if he wanted. I told him I could quit if I wanted, so which would it be? Eventually, he lost the store. I was the last employee he had; no one else could bear to work for him. I stayed until the end, and I even helped him sell the furnishings. It was sad for him and for me. I have not heard from him since that time.

Each year, I would travel back to Missouri. For ten years, each time I came to Jefferson City, I visited a prison. I know non-correctional people will have a hard time understanding this. RCC, my beloved institution, was in ruins. I did go to CMCC; however, Boss II (my friend) there had passed away at a young age. The institution was eventually closed down to make way for newer prisons. MSP closed its doors in 2004. The place was so old it was not financially feasible to keep it open. It is now owned by the city and is a tourist attraction. Tours are given by former employees. The tours seem to be profitable. The old prison was also on the TV show, *Ghost Stories*. I can tell you there are no ghosts at MSP, only memories and stories for many staff and inmates. It holds bittersweet memories for me.

Now there are several new maximum security prisons across the state including the Jefferson City Correctional Center (JCCC), the replacement for MSP. After it opened, I would go there. I had several friends working at this prison. It has a beautiful plaque in the main hallway with the names of people who worked there. The first time I viewed it, my picture was not in the plaque. I contacted the warden. He told me I must have been missed. He asked me to send an older picture of me to him. He would make sure it was placed in the plaque. He kept his word. I felt good to be among my peers who toiled there.

Now, after twelve-plus years, I haven't been visiting a prison when I go home. Most of the people working in the two prisons in the area are new. I feel sad to not visit a prison. Prison life was such a part of me. I feel I have finally lost an old friend. I am sure most of the female employees in DOC now do not have any idea who I am or what I represent. I am one of many unknown women who made it possible for other women to hold non-traditional positions. The reason I have written this book is to validate what I have accomplished. I want to inform all readers of what women have endured in order to rise within the ranks. There is so much prison hype in Jefferson City, there is even a restaurant/bar named "Prison Brews" located near the old MSP. I enjoy going there.

My story of the criminal justice field does continue on in Williamsburg. Sometime in 2004, I saw an article in the local newspaper about a county corrections office. I didn't even know it existed. I quickly sent my résumé, with several letters of recommendation, to the agency director, who called me to come in for an interview. She told me they had no open positions at that time, but she asked if I would consider volunteering in the large regional jail. The jail had a job readiness program sponsored by her organization. Reentry in Virginia was just beginning. I knew that could be a foot in the door, so I said

I would volunteer. I was still closing the health food store at that time.

I started as a volunteer in 2004. I interviewed inmates in the jail in order to find out some of what they would need when released. I spoke at the job readiness program about what our organization could do for them. The jail was very different from a prison, but some things were the same. Basic rules were the same. Gates clanged. Smells were similar. Inmates did not have the freedom of the prison or many of the programs or staff. There were no paid caseworkers, psychologists, substance abuse counselors, etc. A wide variety of volunteers/agencies were used to fill the gaps when staff and programs were lacking. I began to feel at home. Staff at the jail welcomed me.

Soon after, the director began to pay me an hourly wage for my time. The hours I put in were very few. My pay at that time was not what I had hoped for. It was the going rate for service workers in the area. In late 2004 or early 2005, I was approached about a sixteen-hour-per-week probation officer position. The hourly pay was much greater than I'd ever received in Virginia. I would still continue to work in the jail part time. I jumped at the chance to be directly working with offenders again. Now I work with them on the outside rather than the inside. There were two obstacles I had to overcome. One was remembering I was not an administrator but a low-ranking employee. This has been a problem for me since I retired. The other was learning to call a person on probation a client rather than offender/ex-inmate. I think now I can separate the names properly.

My duties are ever changing. I now have the large title of Transitional Services Jail Liaison. I shortened it to Reentry

Coordinator. The year 2012 was the big year for reentry. The federal and state governments are on the bandwagon. I am now working more in the jail and less with regular clients. I have also learned the duties of a pre-trial officer. I am not sure I like the changes. I like one-on-one and follow-up work. I am a part of a several committees and a reentry board. It is exciting; however, the progress in this area of Virginia is slow. Some residents pretend the homeless are not here. Most locals don't even think of a prisoner leaving the jail. You can see them walking on the highway with their plastic bags over their arms after they've been released. I will say there are many organizations, churches, and individuals who are putting forth great efforts to help those released from jails or prisons. The town in Missouri where I worked was accustomed to prisons. The town supported most of the efforts.

I have steadily continued this work to the present time. I love working with the clients. Communication with them brings me great satisfaction. I have over two hundred hours of training under my belt since I moved to Virginia. Among them are motivational interviewing, evidence-based practices, case planning, and all the other modern terms for putting the criminogenic needs of the client first. I also learned how to check urine for drugs. This was a first for me. It is not the most pleasant duty I have. Many probation officers in Virginia were punitive in their thinking, but that's not a problem for me. The Boss, who was progressive and ahead of his time, trained me well.

Every inmate who came into the Department of Corrections in Missouri had to develop a personalized plan with his/her caseworker. This idea is the same as the present case planning. I disagree with some of the techniques used in interviewing the clients, because the questions can be methodical and also condescending, in my opinion. I use the techniques when applicable but do not conduct an interview in a counseling manner. I try to develop a trust and commonality with the client. I let them know that I know where they're coming from. If I have a young, black probationer, I make sure I've already learned some of the music. One young man came in who loved to rap. He was also a great admirer of President Obama. One of his homework assignments was to write a positive rap song about the President. He came in proudly at the next office visit with the assignment complete. The age gap vanished.

Another client appeared to be a white supremacist. His tattoos and outspokenness were great indicators. He had been to prison several times. He and I struck a commonality because of the prison experiences of both of us. I deal again with gang members and "wannabes". I treat them with respect. I work with many single mothers and many young men who have been raised without a father. They are of special interest to me.

You might think that my age, now that I'm a senior, could present a problem with probationers. This doesn't usually happen. We are all more alike than we might think. With drug addicts, I talk about the addiction of nicotine I finally freed myself from eighteen years ago. I can "talk the talk" of the streets even though I have not "walked the walk." It made me a bit sad when a young man told me he felt safe in my office. He had many psychological problems to work through. I did not judge him. One female client complimented me because she said, "You do not judge." Family members of the clients usually respect me. I still cling to my training of fair, firm, consistent, and without judgment. How can anyone judge? There, but for the grace of God, go I or my family. I remember when I was poorly paid I sometimes wrote a check before the money was deposited in the bank. That action was technically a crime.

Some of the work has become harder. I have a condition called macular degeneration; so far, with medical techniques, I manage. I know someday the computer will be problem for me. The cartilage in my knees is almost gone. Sometimes, on a busy day, it is hard for me to walk the long hallways of the jail or walk to and from my office with the clients. Still, I cannot imagine giving up my work with the offenders. There is so much to do and so many who need help.

My new position was not without events. Some who work in the probation/parole field did not understand my prior experience or administrative duties. Recently the Virginia Department of Corrections placed parole officers in the prisons to help with reentry. For as long as I can remember, Missouri had an institutional parole officer in every institution. The local parole officers were in the field. Some of my colleagues at one time tried to test me and my abilities. I believe now I have stood my ground, and I seem to be accepted for the most part. Still, I relate more to an officer who's had jail experience and the staff of the local jail. I put security first. Some of my ideas are thought to be different. I have sometimes seen politics surface again but at my age, I do not care.

I have had problems with the local community seeing my point when I make a remark or suggestion. They think I appear negative or harsh. I am neither. I go backwards from the worst-case scenario to the best, as I was taught. An example of these thoughts came to light when a committee was discussing a new overnight homeless shelter. I was concerned that maybe some of the security had been overlooked. One volunteer told me he had spent two nights in a shelter, and the second night he slept like a baby. I would never sleep like a baby in a homeless shelter—it's not always that different from a prison. Some of the same residents are there. Mental health problems abound among the homeless. There are no places left to house them to control their medications.

When I worked in the Juvenile Attention Center in Missouri on weekends, I learned what problem teens are all about. I do not choose to work with juveniles. This type of population must be approached with caution and concern. Many I worked with had no parenting at all. I was talking to a teen-age girl one day. She was excited that her father was coming to visit. In the same breath, she told me her daddy loved her and added he had raped her. Instances like this were too hard for me to accept.

CONCLUDING THOUGHTS

How can I conclude a story which has, of this writing, not yet been concluded? How can I end a career in criminal justice when I don't want it to be over? How long will I continue to be physically able to share my knowledge with those who have come after me in the field? These are questions I cannot answer. I don't even want to try.

As I look back on the seventy years of my life, I am grateful to God. He has blessed me in so many ways. I thank him daily. My father was taken away at young age, but God also blessed me with everything I needed: food, shelter, good health, safety, and a mother who was with me every step of the way. Someone said she was my strength. She was and continues to be. I prayed when I was young that I would not be left an orphan. I wasn't—my mother lived to be eighty-eight years old.

I was blessed with a wonderful son. God gave us all we needed to make it in this world. I would never say it was easy; it was very hard. After some terrible teen years, my son is now a scientist. He also was able to find the means to provide for his family. There were times along the way when none of us knew if we would eat, but we did. I was also blessed with a wonderful daughter-in-law who has put up with my quirks and opinions all of these years. I know that could not have been easy.

My older granddaughter is married to a great young man. She has her dad's smarts in math and science and is pursuing a PhD in chemistry at University of Virginia in Charlottesville. My younger granddaughter has abilities in writing, photography, and most of the things I liked when I was young, although she will not agree. She is pursuing a degree in mass communications at Virginia Commonwealth University in Richmond. The latest blessing is my great-granddaughter, Haylee. She has given more meaning to my life. I had never thought of being a great-grandmother. I love watching her grow and I have no doubt she will go on to do great things. She is just following in the family footsteps.

As a child, I was introverted and obese. I amused myself by reading, beginning with comic books. In my teen years, after losing eighty pounds on my own diet, I became probably too social. I forgot to do the best I could do in high school. Knowing I needed to be a responsible parent, I knew I could only support my son with a nontraditional job for women in the sixties.

The experience in my life which changed my personality the most was corrections. I became outspoken, persistent, and opinionated, and I developed some bad traits. My language can sometimes match the language of the inmates. I learned to have a "sick" sense of humor—I laughed when an inmate had a jar of Vaseline in a spot he could not remove it from. There were so many negatives; I had to laugh at abnormal situations. If I didn't, I would have cried.

I became streetwise. It was fun to go to the ghetto of St. Louis City to look for an escaped inmate. I had the knowledge to go on the streets to buy drugs if I chose to. Thank God, again, I don't drink at all, and I have never used illegal drugs. My son tells me I feel too comfortable with society's rejects. I understand them. Much of my knowledge cannot be understood by the friends and acquaintances I have met here. I miss my corrections friends and stories.

I am sad to conclude this book. I hope readers do not find it too harsh or bold. I just gave my own opinions about what happened as I moved from the lowest position at MSP to one of middle management and administrative duties. Some younger women may not understand what I have tried to say to them. Remember, young women, I was your predecessor. I paved the way for you. We are not there yet, but it is much better. My blood, sweat, and tears helped other women to move up the career ladder in corrections. I broke the barriers, as I am sure many other women across the country, and before me, did also. I commend them all.

My son and I proved the statistics wrong. I successfully reared a son without a male figure in the home. He became successful despite roadblocks. We both earned our way in totally different fields. My mother passed down to us her exceptional work ethic. I am proud of that.

I also love my chosen field, even with all the heartaches, disappointments, and trials. I thank God he put me where I was supposed to be. I feel sure I have been a part of changing people's lives. I am proud of my work and my ability to work with the people society has chosen to ignore for so many years. I applaud all of my colleagues for their work in the criminal justice field. It is ever-changing. I applaud all of the men and women who have pulled themselves out of the justice system and/or addictions and thus have gone on to be productive citizens. I want to continue in this field and continue to contribute. What else can I say?

INSTITUTION IDENTIFICATION:

Missouri State Penitentiary, MSP

Renz Correctional Center, RCC

Central Missouri Correctional Center, CMCC

Jefferson City Correctional Center, JCCC

Algoa Correctional Center, ACC

Fulton Reception and Diagnostic Center, FRDC

Department of Corrections, DOC

Division of Adult Institutions, DAI

TRAINING MISSOURI DEPARTMENT OF CORRECTIONS 1966–2000

(PARTIAL LIST)

ADVANCED TRAINING (1974)—RANKED FIRST OF TEN

FINGERPRINT SEMINAR (1977)

BOOMERANG (1977)

CRIMINAL CODE UPDATE (1977, 1979)

EMERGING WOMEN IN MANAGEMENT (1978)

PRE-EMPLOYMENT INTERVIEW TRAINING (1979)

MISSOURI CORRECTIONAL ASSOCIATION (1979, 1985)

PRINCIPLES OF SUPERVISION (1980)

EXECUTIVE MANAGEMENT TRAINING (1982)

THE FEMALE OFFENDER (1982)

CLASSIFICATION SYSTEM TRAINING (1983)

INTERVIEW TEAM TRAINING (1987)

EFFECTIVE LEADERSHIP (1987)

E-SQUAD LEADER TRAINING (1987)

FOOD SERVICE MANAGER'S TRAINING (1987)

FLSA TRAIN THE TRAINER (1987)

RESPOND NORMALLY—BIZARRE BEHAVIOR (1987)

BELIEF/PRACTICE—RIGHT WING (1987)

NARCOTICS/INVESTIGATIVE TECHNIQUES (1987)

UNION RESOLUTION TRAINING (1987)

SECURITY TRAINING (1988)

FIREFIGHTING TECHNIQUES (1988)

POLICY AND PROCEDURE TRAINING (1988)

AIDS TRAINING (1988)

CORRECTIONAL FOOD SERVICE COURSE (1987)

BASIC HUMAN RELATIONS SKILLS (1988)

EFFECTIVE INTERACTION/ANGRY AND RESISTANT CLIENT (1988)

RACIAL AND SEXUAL HARASSMENT TRAINING (1988)

PORNOGRAPHY AND ITS EFFECTS (1988)

DISCRIMINATION SENSITIVITY TRAINING (1989)

POLICY AND PROCEDURE II (1989)

E-SQUAD EMERGENCY PROCEDURES (1989)

HEALTH CARE (1988)

AIDS—NEW MATERIAL (1989)

SECURITY TRANSITIONS TRAINING (1989)

CHALLENGES OF MANAGING THE WORKFORCE (1990)

GRIEVANCE PROCEDURE TRAINING (1990)

NOTE: THIS BOOK HAS BEEN EDITED BY CREATESPACE.

Made in the USA
Charleston, SC
19 March 2013